'A wealth of practical tips to help teachers support children with Specific Learning Difficulties (SpLDs). Diana Hudson explains what the challenges are, how they affect learning and provides simple strategies for the classroom. This book should be compulsory reading for all teachers and TAs, and parents will find it useful too.'

– *Alison Thompson, author of* The Boy From Hell: Life with a Child with ADHD *and founder of ADHD kids*

'Di Hudson's book, with its practical and common-sense approach to SpLDs, is ideal in helping the busy, overworked class teacher to understand the needs of students with SpLDs, and also enables them to find workable strategies to help all students reach their full potential.'

– *Louise Green, MSc in Human Communications, RSA Dip in SpLD, Cert. Ed, APC (Patoss), TPC (Patoss)*

Specific Learning Difficulties – What Teachers Need to Know

of related interest

Asperger Syndrome – What Teachers Need to Know
Second Edition
Matt Winter with Clare Lawrence
ISBN 978 1 84905 203 0
eISBN 978 0 85700 430 7

Common SENse for the Inclusive Classroom
How Teachers Can Maximise Existing Skills to Support Special
Educational Needs
Richard Hanks
ISBN 978 1 84905 057 9
eISBN 978 0 85700 247 1

Kids in the Syndrome Mix of ADHD, LD, Autism Spectrum,
Tourette's, Anxiety, and More!
The one-stop guide for parents, teachers, and other professionals
Martin L. Kutscher
ISBN 978 1 84905 967 1
eISBN 978 0 85700 882 4

Can I tell you about Dyslexia?
A guide for friends, family and professionals
Alan M. Hultquist
Illustrated by Bill Tulp
ISBN 978 1 84905 952 7
eISBN 978 0 85700 810 7

Can I tell you about Dyspraxia?
A guide for friends, family and professionals
Maureen Boon
Illustrated by Imogen Hallam
ISBN 978 1 84905 447 8
eISBN 978 0 85700 824 4

Can I tell you about OCD?
A guide for friends, family and professionals
Amita Jassi
Illustrated by Sarah Hull
Foreword by Isobel Heyman
ISBN 978 1 84905 381 5
eISBN 978 0 85700 736 0

Specific Learning Difficulties – What Teachers Need to Know

Diana Hudson

Illustrated by Jon English

Jessica Kingsley *Publishers*
London and Philadelphia

First published in 2016
by Jessica Kingsley Publishers
73 Collier Street
London N1 9BE, UK
and
400 Market Street, Suite 400
Philadelphia, PA 19106, USA

www.jkp.com

Copyright © Diana Hudson 2016
Illustrations copyright © Jon English 2016

Front cover image: Jon English.

Disclaimer: Some names and identifying details have been changed to protect the privacy of individuals.

Library of Congress Cataloging in Publication Data
Hudson, Diana, author.
  Specific learning difficulties : what teachers need to know / Diana Hudson ;
illustrated by Jon English.
    pages cm
  Includes bibliographical references and index.
  ISBN 978-1-84905-590-1 (alk. paper)
  1. Learning disabilities--Handbooks, manuals, etc. 2. Learning disabled children--Education--
Handbooks, manuals, etc. I. Title.
  LC4704.H84 2016
  371.9--dc23

                                        2015018536

British Library Cataloguing in Publication Data
A CIP catalogue record for this book is available from the British Library

ISBN 978 1 84905 590 1
eISBN 978 1 78450 046 7

Printed and bound in Great Britain

MIX
Paper from
responsible sources
FSC® C013056

Contents

Acknowledgements

Many people have helped me to get this book from the starting block to completion and I am very grateful for their help, advice and kind words of encouragement.

In particular I would like to thank:

- Jon English, the artist, for bringing the book to life

- Meg Scullion, for spending hours painstakingly sifting through the manuscript and helping to knock it into shape

- Jenny, Michael and Francis Budden-Hinds, for continued support and ideas throughout

- Clare Addison and Kirsten Taylor, for help with editing.

My thanks also go to the following experts who have kindly advised and helped me in the areas shown below:

- Alex Bettey and Gill Dixon, of the Dyspraxia Foundation

- Elizabeth Chacksfield, teaching students with specific learning difficulties

- Bill Colley, educational consultant for special needs autism spectrum disorder/attention deficit hyperactivity disorder

- Neil Cottrell, managing director, LexAble Ltd, also on BDA (British Dyslexia Association) New Technologies Committee

- Louise Green, specialist assessor and advisor on specific learning difficulties
  - Professor Peter Hill, child and adolescent psychiatrist
  - Clare Holland and Jon Nesbitt, behavioural optometrists
  - Amita Jassi, clinical psychologist and obsessive compulsive disorder specialist
  - Professor Paul Moorcraft for his insight into dyscalculia
  - Alison Thompson, founder of ADHD Kids
  - Patience Thomson, for inspiration and guidance during my time as a special educational needs coordinator.

Thanks also to the kind and helpful staff at Jessica Kingsley Publishers for their support.

Finally my love and thanks go to my husband, Mike, who has kept me buoyant throughout this book-writing venture and encouraged me to sit down and get on with it, and also to our children Jenny, Tim, Jessica and Kay for their support, making me laugh and stopping me from taking myself too seriously.

Introduction

This book is written for busy classroom teachers in secondary schools. It aims to give an insight into the minds, strengths and weaknesses of students who have Specific Learning Difficulties (SpLDs), and to provide an armoury of practical ideas to teach them more effectively. It is not designed to be read from cover to cover but to be dipped into selectively.

Students with SpLDs can appear to be able and articulate but they regularly underperform in certain subjects or tasks. Written work may be below the expected standard and they can be disorganised or challenging. Conversely, the same students can be inventive, perceptive, creative and talented. The challenge for teachers is to enable these young people to find ways around their problems and to harness their talents.

Estimates suggest that in a typical class of 30 there will be one, probably two, students with an SpLD. They are found in all types of schools and at all levels of ability. Sadly for some of these pupils, their particular learning difficulty will not be identified and they will remain unsupported. Their intelligence and potential can be underestimated and there is a danger that they will leave school with poor self-esteem and lower grades and aspirations than they could have achieved.

The most common SpLDs are outlined in this book, and every chapter includes teaching and classroom management tips which will, I hope, be helpful when planning lessons and activities. In some cases the wider whole-school policy of student care is considered.

Three medically diagnosed conditions that affect the learning and behaviour of teenagers are also included in this book. This is because they often occur concurrently with other SpLDs, and teaching methods can be adapted to support them.

The format is as follows:

- ○ Chapter 1 considers the brain and learning. It introduces SpLDs and many of the terms that are used when considering learning styles, processing information and making informed decisions.

- ○ Chapters 2–8 each cover a different specific condition.

- ○ Chapters 9 and 10 focus on organisational skills and exams for all the groups of students with an SpLD as their problems and needs overlap.

I hope that you will enjoy this book and find it a helpful source of ideas. Students with SpLDs can be among the most interesting, challenging and exciting people to teach. Many have talents, abilities and an intellectual capacity that will allow them to become highly successful in their chosen career. As a teacher, it is a joy to be able to help them unlock their potential.

Chapter 1

Brains That Work a Little Differently

Introducing Specific Learning Difficulties

* What are Specific Learning Difficulties?
* How do we learn best?
* Different learning styles
* Active or passive learning?
* Processing speed
* Short- and long-term memory
* Attention span
* Executive function skills
* Hearing and vision
* Specific Learning Difficulties: daunting or exciting?
* Remember, you are not alone
* Key points

Within any class of students there will be a range of academic ability, personality, strengths and weaknesses. Usually students will perform in a fairly consistent manner across all subjects but there may be a few who are very good at some things but perform surprisingly badly at others. It is this disparity that identifies people who have Specific Learning Difficulties (SpLDs). As teachers it is important to understand how these students think in order to help them learn effectively and thrive.

What are Specific Learning Difficulties?

The term 'Specific Learning Difficulties' has been defined as 'a particular difficulty in one area of learning in a child who performs satisfactorily in other areas' (Worthington 2003). These problems often run in families and they occur in all racial groups and economic backgrounds.

People cannot be cured and they don't 'grow out of' their difficulties, but they can be taught to find a range of alternative coping strategies to help to them to take in and retain information, pass exams and become successful adults. They usually have many talents and skills in other areas which can make a considerable impact in their chosen career.

If sympathetic and adaptable teachers can help these students to find their strengths and learning styles it can make a huge difference and enable them to blossom.

The most common SpLDs which may be found in mainstream classrooms are:

- o *Dyslexia:* problems with reading, writing and spelling
- o *Dyscalculia:* problems with numbers
- o *Dysgraphia:* physical problems with handwriting
- o *Dyspraxia:* problems with movement and coordination
- o *Attention deficit hyperactivity disorder (ADHD):* short attention span, lively and impulsive behaviour
- o *Autism spectrum disorders (ASD) such as Asperger Syndrome:* social and communication difficulties, awkwardness in social interaction, factual unimaginative speech, and a preoccupation with very narrow interests

○ *Obsessive compulsive disorder (OCD):* unfounded worries and fears (obsessions) that lead to repetitive behaviour patterns (compulsions).

Each SpLD mentioned will be outlined in this book, with a description of the indicators to look out for and common strengths to encourage. Classroom strategies to help these students will be included. *All these conditions vary in severity along a continuum from mild to severe, so no two students will be the same.* Just to confuse matters further, there is also considerable co-existence of the conditions mentioned and each learner will have their own 'cocktail' of problems (See Figure 1.1). For example, some students with dyslexia may also have dyscalculia or dyspraxia, others will not. In this book I have outlined each of the conditions separately, but you may need to dip into several chapters if a student has a 'mix' of difficulties. This general overlap is illustrated in Figure 1.1.

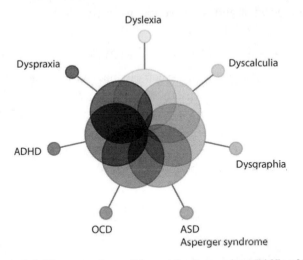

Figure 1.1 The overlap of Specific Learning Difficulties

More information can be found in the Appendix, which shows a summary of the most common symptoms for each disorder.

It is important to try to understand your students' 'mix' and the severity of their problems so that you can work with them to achieve success.

How do we learn best?

We all have strengths and weaknesses and ways that we prefer to learn. I will briefly outline some key points and introduce some terms which are used when describing people who have difficulty in one area of learning.

Left or right brain?

Everyone's brain has two halves which have different roles. They are linked by nerves which allow the two sides of the brain to communicate, but in most of us one side is dominant, making us more left- or right-brained. This will affect our skills, perception and personality. It will also influence what we are good at and how we like to learn.

- - - - - - - **Did you know?** - - - - - - -

Men are generally more left-brained and women right-brained. Does this explain why women often have trouble with parallel parking and men can't multi-task? (Pease and Pease 2001)

- -

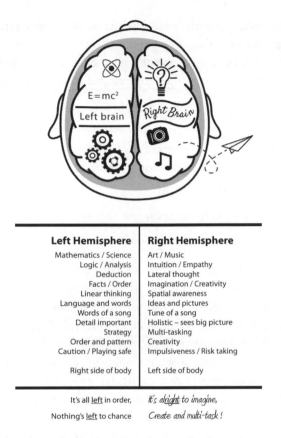

Left Hemisphere	Right Hemisphere
Mathematics / Science	Art / Music
Logic / Analysis	Intuition / Empathy
Deduction	Lateral thought
Facts / Order	Imagination / Creativity
Linear thinking	Spatial awareness
Language and words	Ideas and pictures
Words of a song	Tune of a song
Detail important	Holistic – sees big picture
Strategy	Multi-tasking
Order and pattern	Creativity
Caution / Playing safe	Impulsiveness / Risk taking
Right side of body	Left side of body
It's all <u>left</u> in order,	*It's al<u>right</u> to imagine,*
Nothing's <u>left</u> to chance	*Create and multi-task !*

Figure 1.2 Left and right brain function

Students with SpLDs are often at the extremes of the normal left- and right-brain balance. Students with dyslexia are often very right-brained, creative and imaginative, while those with ASD are much more left-brained, preferring facts, logic and order. This shows the importance of varying class teaching methods and using a variety of ways of delivering information.

As teachers, we are inclined to teach in the way that we like to learn. I am very right-brained so my lessons will often involve film clips, cartoons and craft work, even to A-level biology students. I have to remember that some of my more left-brained students would prefer a fact sheet rather than being told to make a poster.

It is useful to be aware of your own strengths, weaknesses and learning style, and to understand that others may think differently.

Different learning styles

Information is received through three main channels:

- What we see: *visual*
- What we hear: *auditory*
- What we feel: *kinaesthetic.*

Most people have a preferred channel or *learning style*. The most successful lessons are as *multisensory* as possible. This encourages students to use all three learning channels and the lesson material is reinforced in several ways.

It is important to remember that some students with SpLDs may have problems taking in and remembering material presented in one particular way, and so it is vital to use a variety of approaches and learning channels to engage with them.

Sometimes these three learning styles are subdivided further. Auditory can be separated into *verbal* and *musical* as these skills involve different sides of the brain. It is also recognised that some people are sociable with good *interpersonal skills* and they will thrive in group situations. Others will be more solitary and self-reliant and have strong *intrapersonal* skills and they will prefer to work alone.

LEARNING STYLE	HOW THEY LEARN BEST
VISUAL	**Looking and observing** Reading the text, using pictures, diagrams, posters, charts, films, displays, handouts and effective use of colour
AUDITORY	**Listening and speaking** Stories, songs, audio tapes, music, discussions with other students and talking through problems out loud
KINAESTHETIC	**Physical experience** Touching , experimenting, holding, feeling, doing, building, creating models, movement, coordination and using computers

Figure 1.3 Learning styles

--------- Do you say: ---------

a) 'Listen to me' b) 'Watch me' c) 'Copy what I do?'

a) 'I hear what you say' b) 'I see what you mean' c) 'I understand how you feel?'

These phrases indicate our own preferred learning channel. To check yours, try one of the online quizzes listed at the end of this book (see page 220).

It is valuable for teachers to be aware of these preferences for all students but especially for those with SpLDs. All students should, however, be encouraged to work outside their comfort zone sometimes, and this is another advantage of using a multisensory approach.

Above all, try to make your lessons active, stimulating and exciting to keep students engaged.

Active or passive learning?

Active learning is when the students are participating in activities such as group discussions, debating, carrying out experiments, giving presentations or inventing a new teaching resource. The increased learning potential of active learning is clearly demonstrated by the learning graph shown in Figure 1.4.

It will come as no surprise to learn that students retain information better if they are actively involved in their own learning process, rather than being passive recipients of information. It is often easy for us as teachers to slip into the 'lecture style' approach, especially when we are racing to 'get through' the syllabus. However, do try to hand over to the students sometimes. You will be amazed by the results.

Also, an opportunity for active learning often delights students with SpLDs and it can be a time when they really have the chance to shine. They can sometimes produce unusual, exciting and stimulating material, which they can show to their peers. This is good for their self-esteem and we can all enjoy and celebrate their talents.

– – – – – – – – – – **Idea** – – – – – – – – – –

Try getting the students to invent board games or songs linked to a topic. It can be fun.

– –

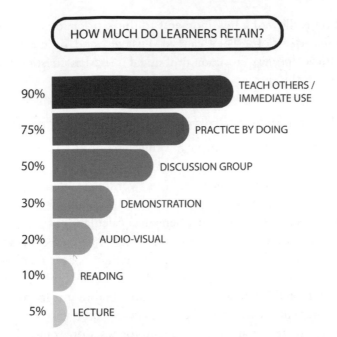

Figure 1.4 Retention of information
(Figures are based on the learning pyramid usually attributed to the NTL (National Training Laboratories) Institute of Applied Behavioral Science in Virginia, USA)

Processing speed

When we take in information that we see, hear or experience physically it takes a little time to think about it and respond. This is called *processing time*. The shorter the processing time, the faster thinking and learning can take place.

Some people are described as having a slow processing speed and so they will take longer to absorb the information and think about a response. This does not reflect their overall intelligence or physical defects with sight or hearing. It is just that the interpretation of the information takes longer.

Students with slow processing speed will, therefore, benefit from having extra time in written tests and should also be allowed a few moments to think prior to answering verbal questions. They can get flustered and be unable to retrieve answers fast enough if asked a sudden question and 'put on the spot'.

Short-term memory (working memory)

Information that is needed only temporarily, such as a shopping list, a set of instructions or the score in tennis, goes into our short-term memory. This 'working' memory is also essential in order not to get 'lost' when carrying out step-by-step procedures such as mathematical calculations.

If a student has a poor short-term memory they will continually forget instructions, meetings, page numbers, equipment, homework, to name but a few. All information must, therefore, be written or recorded before it is forgotten.

Students with short-term memory problems will be unable to revise at the last minute for tests or exams. They will have to commit information to their long-term memory in order to fix it. This will take longer and need greater repetition and reinforcement.

Long-term memory

We build up and retain a bank of knowledge that can be retrieved for many years, owing to our long-term memories. Once material has been committed to long-term memory, it is much more rooted and may even stay with us for life. Even as adults most of us can remember nursery rhymes or expressions that our parents said to us in childhood.

We are often better able to remember information if we can make some mental connection such as a rhyme, mnemonic, musical rhythm or some silly or naughty connotation. This makes it more likely to enter the long-term memory.

Ask any doctor and they are likely to be able to recall at least one dubious rhyme for remembering the names of the cranial nerves.

Attention span

The length of time for which students at secondary school can concentrate on a single activity will vary, but it is a relatively short time, around 15 minutes for teenagers.

It is therefore beneficial to change activity several times within a lesson. Pupils with particular SpLDs such as ADHD have even shorter concentration spans than usual for their age group, and this will affect their ability to learn new material and to perform well. These students can easily become bored and either just 'switch off' or disrupt lessons.

Changing the learning style and pace of the lesson regularly can help to keep students focused. Aim to make progress in short sprints rather than going for a marathon!

Executive function skills

These skills are related to planning and organising, setting targets, learning from experience and controlling impulsive behaviour. Most teenagers have problems in these areas but gradually improve as they move through secondary school. However, students with ADHD, dyspraxia and other SpLDs may have greater difficulty than their peers with organisation and planning. They will probably continue to need help and support in these areas throughout school.

Hearing

A student who has deafness is not classed as having a Specific Learning Difficulty even though they will need special arrangements.

However, conditions such as *glue ear* in young children reduce their hearing accuracy. Even if this physical problem has been remedied, children may have missed an early stage of development when they would have identified sounds made by letters and combinations of letters (phonemes) within words. This can contribute to spelling and reading problems later as they have not heard words accurately in the past. They may miss out syllables when they write, or muddle consonants incorrectly such as p for b. Many children with dyslexia have a history of glue ear in early childhood.

Vision

Students with poor eyesight may require special arrangements but this is not a Specific Learning Difficulty.

However, some students may have problems with *tracking*, which is the ability to coordinate the two eyes to follow words on a line of print. This can cause great difficulty with reading. *Visual stress* is another condition where the eyes do not work correctly together, and this can cause the letters to merge or the lines to jump (see Figure 1.5). Clearly this makes it very difficult to read accurately and to copy from a board. Visual stress and tracking problems can be improved with regular eye exercises and it has also been found that using plastic coloured overlays when reading can help. Strictly speaking, these are not SpLDs but physical problems. It is confusing, though, as some people with visual stress or tracking difficulties also have SpLDs.

If there are any suspicions of visual problems causing a student to copy inaccurately or complain of tired eyes and headaches, it is worth asking a specialist behavioural optometrist to investigate further so that the student can receive the correct support.

Figure 1.5 Two views of visual stress

Specific Learning Difficulties: daunting or exciting?

It is exciting and invigorating to be able to help students with lifelong SpLDs overcome their problems, celebrate their strengths and embrace their successes.

It is sometimes more helpful to think in terms of students having *learning differences* rather than difficulties or disabilities, as they also have many strengths and talents.

- -

Everyone's brain works differently. Why aren't people celebrated for their contributions and not constantly put down for what they find difficult?

Young adult with dyspraxia

- -

I can't emphasise enough how much an understanding and supportive teacher can brighten the outlook and raise the aspirations of students with learning differences. You won't be right all the time but if the students know that you have faith in them and want them to succeed, that is a long way down the road to their success.

The key is to remain cheerful and upbeat and to talk to the students about what helps them the most. Be flexible in your approach and don't be afraid to try out different ideas. Sometimes the most wacky ones work the best!

Remember, you are not alone

There are other professionals in school who help students with SpLDs and advise their teachers, so do not feel that you are alone. Most schools and sixth-form colleges will have a named person who is *head of pastoral care* and each student will have a *year head* and they may also have an *adult mentor*. There is usually a *SENCO* (special educational needs coordinator) whose job it is to make sure that the student's individual needs are catered for by the school. This may include setting up individual lessons with a specialist *learning support teacher* or acting on advice from a student's doctor or physiotherapist. Special arrangements for examinations may need to be made and the SENCO should keep class teachers informed about students' needs and progress. You may also be able to have a *teaching assistant* working with you in the classroom if the student needs more support. Make sure that you discuss any worries with the appropriate person and work as a united team. Remember that you are not solely responsible for dealing with these students' difficulties.

Key points

* We all have different strengths, weaknesses and preferred ways of learning.

* We take in information through our eyes, ears and physical experiences.

* Lessons are most effective if they are multisensory and involve students in active participation.

* Some students have SpLDs which make it harder for them to take in and process information that is presented in one way, but they can usually access it via a different route.

* Students may have problems with concentration span, processing speeds, working memory and organisation.

* Physical problems with vision or hearing are not in themselves SpLDs, but they can be contributory factors.

* Having SpLDs does not affect the overall intelligence of the student.

* A cheerful, proactive and sympathetic teacher can make all the difference.

Chapter 2

Dyslexia

* What is dyslexia?

* How can I spot a student with dyslexia?

* Common indicators

* Common strengths

* How can I help in the classroom?

* Individual help

* Key points

What is dyslexia?

People with dyslexia have *difficulty with the written language* and so they have problems with reading, writing and spelling.

Dyslexia has been defined as a 'difficulty in interpretation of the written language in a person who has no visual impairment, hearing impairment or intellectual impairment' (Worthington 2003).

Dyslexia occurs across the full range of intellectual abilities. It is thought to affect up to 10 per cent of the population, with a severity varying along a continuum from mild to severe (British Dyslexia Association). It can affect both boys and girls.

The term 'developmental dyslexia' is sometimes used; this means that the person is born with the condition, and that it has not occurred as a result of an illness or accident. It cannot be cured but coping strategies can be learned.

**Where does the
- - - - - - name come from? - - - - - -**

Dys comes from the Greek word meaning *difficulty*.

Lexis also comes from the Greek word meaning *word*.

So dyslexia means *difficulty with words*.

- -

Dyslexia often runs in families, which suggests that there might be a genetic link. It sometimes occurs with allergic conditions such as asthma, eczema or hayfever.

Brain imaging techniques show that people with dyslexia process information differently from others. They tend to think more in pictures than in words and make rapid lateral connections (Schnep 2014). This can be very advantageous in some circumstances and walks of life.

Hearing problems in early childhood, such as glue ear, or visual weakness such as eye tracking difficulties, do not themselves cause dyslexia but they can be contributory factors (see Chapter 1).

How can I spot a student with dyslexia?

Dyslexia is often discovered because of a discrepancy between a student's good oral ability and their mediocre to poor performance on paper.

Look out for a student who makes sensible and intelligent contributions in class but consistently comes out with test and exam results which are lower than expected, despite hard work. They might also appear to make 'silly' mistakes due to misreading questions or instructions.

Common indicators

DOWNSIDES

Students with dyslexia will show some of the indicators listed below, but not all of them, so it can be confusing. Remember that this can be further complicated as some students may have other Specific Learning Difficulties (SpLDs) as well.

Reading

- Slow reading speed.
- Reading is often inaccurate.
- Will not always understand what they have read as they are concentrating on deciphering the words, so may miss the overall meaning.
- Reading inaccuracies increase under pressure. Liable to make more mistakes in tests.
- Will substitute a similar looking word often starting with the same letter. For example, 'silky pyjamas' could become 'silly pyjamas'.
- Difficulty with written comprehension, often due to misreading words, or missing out key words in the text.
- Daunted by large chunks of texts and small print.
- Letter reversal in reading words or numbers such as reading 'sing' for 'sign' or '28' for '82'.
- Dislikes reading out loud as hesitant and inaccurate. Worried about being laughed at.

Spelling

- Inconsistent spelling of the same word, often within a single piece of writing.
- Difficulty with phonology (hearing the sounds in words). May miss out syllables of words, for example 'diffulty' for 'difficulty'.
- May confuse consonants, for example g and k or b and p.

My daughter called potatoes 'botatoes' for years!

Author

- Letter reversal in spelling similar to reading, for example writing brian for brain. This can also occur with writing numbers, which causes difficulty with mathematics.
- Can do well in spelling tests of pre-determined words but spelling 'goes to pieces' when writing an account, as concentration is on the content rather than the spelling.
- Can learn a spelling one day and forget it the next.
- Names of people and places are often misspelt and variable.

Note-taking

- Cannot copy accurately from a board. May copy spellings incorrectly, miss out words or jump lines.
- Cannot keep up with dictation.
- Inaccuracies in notes taken in class, especially in a foreign language or with chemical symbols such as $C_6H_{12}O_6$.

- ° Unable to process and understand information at the same time as writing down notes.

Written work

- ° Slow writing speed.
- ° Poor quality in terms of spelling and punctuation.
- ° Unable to think about the content and spelling at the same time, so if the content is good, the spelling can be poor. Conversely, if the student's concentration flow is disrupted by thinking about spelling, then the content is likely to be stilted.
- ° Written piece may be much shorter and simpler than expected as the student will avoid certain words if they are unsure of the spelling and stick to 'safe' short words.
- ° Capital letters may be used randomly throughout a piece of writing.
- ° Writing may be difficult to read as letters such as a, d, g and q may not be fully formed.
- ° Difficulty organising thoughts clearly and logically, so essays may ramble.
- ° May fail to answer the question, either due to misreading the question itself, failing to understand it or due to lateral thinking causing a drift away from the topic.

Mathematics

Some students with dyslexia may be good at mathematics but make errors when interpreting questions.

- ° Misunderstanding questions – maths vocabulary is quite extensive and can be confusing.
- ° Confusing symbols such as + with x and ÷ with –.

- Not reading instructions properly.

- Algebra can be especially difficult if letters such as b, d, p, q, are used.

- Short-term memory problems cause difficulty retaining numbers long enough for the next step of a calculation.

- Difficulty remembering a process involving a series of steps.

Some students might also have dyscalculia (see Chapter 3) but this is not always the case.

Concentration

- Can get distracted easily.

- Often has a short concentration span.

- Makes rapid lateral mental leaps and connections, so can go widely off topic – 'grasshopper mind'.

- Thoughts are often disconnected and not organised or sequential.

Slow processing speed

- Takes longer to answer questions either verbally or in writing. Sometimes this is due to having to change the information mentally into pictures before it can be decoded and worked on.

- Liable to panic under pressure and mind 'goes blank', even with something they know well.

Poor short-term memory

- Problems remembering instructions.

- Difficulty retaining numbers for calculations.

- Difficulty remembering what to write down.

Learning information

o Unable to revise quickly and 'cram' for tests due to a poor short-term memory.

o Takes much longer to learn as things have to be committed to long-term memory.

o Struggles to find effective revision techniques.

Tests and exams

o Can underachieve, causing a discrepancy between verbal performance and written test performance.

o Difficulty organising thoughts clearly and logically for long answers and essays.

o Runs out of time.

o Panics.

o Doesn't read the question properly, so makes apparently 'careless' mistakes.

Organisation

o Forgets instructions or directions.

o Poor sense of direction so gets lost easily.

o Confusion of left and right.

o Can misread timetables and instructions and has difficulty telling the time.

o Gets distracted and forgets the time.

o Forgets to bring equipment, books, notes, homework.

o Loses belongings.

o Confuses names of places and people, especially if they begin with the same letter.

Sensitive, emotional responses

- May feel upset and humiliated in class.
- Will take comments to heart. Upset by criticism.
- Easily discouraged, leading to low self-esteem.
- Sensitive and can lack self-confidence.
- Can be daunted by situations or complex tasks.
- Can decide to play the class jester to gain credit among peers and to give an 'excuse' for not doing so well.

Fatigue

- Generally has to put more effort into keeping up with work and this leads to increased tiredness, stress and anxiety.

Common strengths

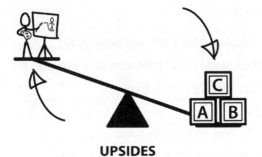

UPSIDES

- Innovative and imaginative thinker
- Good visualisation and spatial skills
- Often creative: good sense of colour and texture, may excel at art, design and photography

- Thinks in pictures, which is quicker and more multidirectional than thinking in words
- Good verbally
- Can be very humorous
- May be good at the performing arts
- Holistic, sees the whole picture
- Can multi-task
- Intuitive problem solver
- Often hard working and tenacious
- High emotional intelligence, empathetic
- Good interpersonal skills
- Valuable and supportive team member
- Entrepreneurial

How can I help in the classroom?

Your attitude is important. Be supportive and upbeat and let any students with dyslexia know that you understand their difficulties. Tell them that you realise they are intelligent and you are expecting them to reach the same goals as the others but their learning strategies may have to be a little different.

Remember that it will take students with dyslexia longer to interpret written questions and to write the answers. Do not expect them to write as much in a set time; they will probably qualify for extra time in tests and exams.

Work with the student to devise successful learning methods. Keep cheerful and be willing to try new approaches. A friendly manner and a sense of humour will make a huge difference.

Seating

Make sure that they sit near the front. This has several advantages:

- They can see the board clearly which will aid reading.
- They are more likely to keep engaged with the lesson and not get distracted.
- You can see their work easily and know whether they are keeping up.
- You can check that information and homework instructions are written down correctly.

Reading

- Always remember that students with dyslexia will take longer to read a text.
- They may also not be able to process the content at the same time as reading.
- Reading accuracy may be poor so encourage them to read instructions slowly, twice.
- Try printing on different coloured backgrounds. It is worth experimenting. They will tell you what works best for them.
- Use a large, clear font.
- Question papers should be well spaced out. Avoid giving students with dyslexia questions which are reduced in size to save paper.

Reading out loud

This can be a major source of panic, stress and embarrassment for some students. They will dread the moment when they are asked to read out loud.

○ Do not suddenly ask them to read out loud.

○ Some students will be happy to read if they have had a chance to see the passage in advance. If this is the case, identify a piece which they can look through before they read.

○ A larger print copy of a text is sometimes easier to read.

○ Many students with dyslexia are good actors, presenters and orators but have trouble sight reading. Give them the text in advance. (Some very talented actors with dyslexia have to learn the audition scripts.)

Spelling

○ Create a list of key spellings for each topic.

○ Students could make a vocabulary book or glossary.

○ Use colour to liven up vocabulary lists, especially in foreign languages. Perhaps nouns could be on one colour paper, verbs on another.

○ Mnemonics can be brilliant for difficult spellings. If they are funny they are more memorable. Look up some for your subject or get the students to make some up.

○ Use any tricks or jokes you can think of to help fix the spelling of difficult words in your own subject.

- -

It is synthesis not sinthesis as scientists always ask why (Y)!

- -

o A spell checker is useful for written assignments, but make sure the student is aware that it will not recognise spelling errors if they make a recognisable word in another context. Phrases such as 'The Duck of Wellington' or 'The Canterbury Tails' will pass unchanged.

- -

The world is full of amazing orgasms.

Year 7 biology student

- -

Giving notes in class

o Ideally give out printed notes. Notes with gaps to fill in are often a good compromise. These can be highlighted and personalised with diagrams or annotations but the writing process is much less arduous. You also know that the students have the correct material to learn from.

o If you are handwriting on a board make sure your own writing is clear, large and easy to read.

o Use different colours for each row or block of writing, so that students are less likely to jump rows.

o Let them sit next to a willing, reliable, clear writing 'buddy' from whom they can copy.

o Dictation: try to avoid this if possible but if you have to dictate, always write up any key words or awkward spellings on the board, and don't go too fast.

o Remember that students with dyslexia are unlikely to be able to process or understand the information at the same time as they are copying from the board or from dictation.

○ Check their work regularly, as there are likely to be many errors.

○ Students with severe dyslexia may be able to record the lesson electronically and listen to it again later. Printed notes should be given as well, though, to avoid hours of copying up after the lessons.

Table 2.1 PowerPoint dos and don'ts

DO	DO NOT
Use a large font size	Use a small font size to fit lots of information onto one slide
Use a clear, simple font	Use fancy writing
Use double spacing	Crowd information
Keep slides simple: one point per slide is enough	Put too much information on each slide
Include colour diagrams or cartoons	Just have writing
Vary the background colour and colour of the writing, such as yellow writing on blue	Use just black writing on a white background
Read the writing out loud to the students and explain the slides further	Talk about other things when the students are trying to read and understand
Keep the slides lively and fun	Make the slides boring
Let the students read the slides through once before making any notes	Expect students to make notes on the first reading

Type of font

- Use a large font size.
- Keep the font simple and clear. Avoid 'character' fonts and ones with serifs.
- Use double spacing.

- - - - - **Preferred font types** - - - - -

Arial

Calibri

Trebuchet

Comic Sans

Century Gothic

- -

Making worksheets (see Figure 2.1)

- Keep sentences short and clear.
- Space information out well: use double spacing.
- Use a large (12 or 14 point) clear font.
- Break up the page with bold headings, subheadings and indentations.
- Use bullet points.
- Add diagrams, cartoons and other visual markers.
- Use colour – although this may be expensive it is excellent if you can use it.
- Print on coloured paper.
- Make the worksheets clear and attractive.

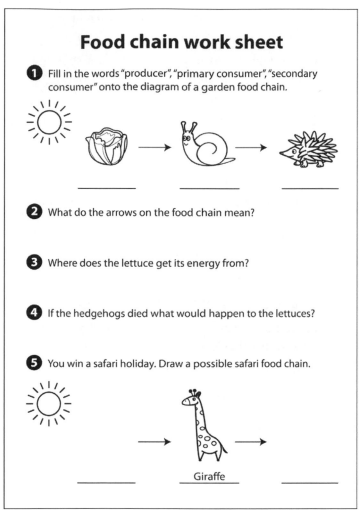

Food chain work sheet

1 Fill in the words "producer", "primary consumer", "secondary consumer" onto the diagram of a garden food chain.

2 What do the arrows on the food chain mean?

3 Where does the lettuce get its energy from?

4 If the hedgehogs died what would happen to the lettuces?

5 You win a safari holiday. Draw a possible safari food chain.

Giraffe

Figure 2.1 Example of a worksheet

Mathematics (see Chapter 3)

- o Read examples out loud as well as writing them on the board.
- o Give a vocabulary list with meanings.

- Try to use letters that look very different from each other.

- Go through an example for the class showing the layout and all the steps of the working out.

- If you are expecting the students to copy down the example, have one printed on a sheet to give to students with dyslexia. (It is less embarrassing if you can give a copy to all students, but this may depend on the school's policy.)

- Teach with visual aids and in a multisensory way.

Studying set texts

People with dyslexia are holistic and like an idea of the 'big picture' before studying the detail.

- Give an overview of the story at the outset.

- Let students know in advance the text or chapters to read so that they can do so before the lesson.

- Is there a larger print version of the book available?

- Is the book available in an unedited audio version?

- Film versions can be useful to give an overview of the plot and bring the characters to life, but remind students that they may differ from the original text.

- - - - - - **A word of caution** - - - - - -

Much as we all enjoyed Colin Firth's portrayal of Mr Darcy in the BBC film of 1995, there is actually no wet shirt scene in Jane Austen's *Pride and Prejudice!*

- -

- Illustrations or diagrams showing the relationships between the characters can be a useful visual aid.

- Try to make the book, poem or passage come alive and go into long-term memory, with theatre visits, acting out sections of the stories in the students' own words, dressing up or having debates from different characters' perspectives.
- How about converting a poem to a rap or song?

Essay writing, course work and projects (see Chapter 9)

These can be very daunting as students with dyslexia feel overwhelmed by perceived 'big' tasks. They tend to see the enormity of the whole project rather than being able to break it down into small, achievable goals.

You can help a great deal by dividing the task into smaller manageable 'chunks' and giving dates when different sections are due. Outline what you are expecting in terms of sections to be completed, approximate word count, and time frame. Ask for each section to be handed in so you can check that the students are on target.

Setting homework

- Set homework early in the lesson.
- Keep instructions clear.
- Give guidance about the length of time you expect students to take.
- Remember that it may take a student with dyslexia a lot longer to complete a piece of work, so indicate what is essential and what could be tackled 'if time'.
- Say clearly when homework should be handed in and where to put it.
- Ideally have the homework task written out on a handout, including page numbers and questions.

If the students write it down themselves, check for accuracy.

○ Can the homework details be recorded electronically? Some schools will let students write or dictate their homework onto a mobile phone.

○ Is there a school intranet where homework details could be placed?

○ Homework books are sometimes useful as parents can see them, if the student remembers to take them home.

○ It is useful to have the number of another member of the group who could be phoned if needed to clarify the homework in the evening.

Enjoyable homework for students with dyslexia

Sometimes set imaginative homework tasks which allow students with dyslexia to use their talents. Teachers could ask students to:

○ Draw a series of pictures or cartoons to illustrate the work.

○ Annotate a picture that you provide.

○ Make up a song/poem/rap/advertisement.

○ Plan a debate about an issue.

○ Make up a game, word search, crossword puzzle (I suggest you check first that the spellings are correct for these!)

○ Prepare a short dramatic presentation.

○ Record a short voice play or monologue.

○ Make a short film.

○ Make a model.

Marking homework

o Mark for content, not spelling. Remember that there is often a disparity between academic ability and written English. 'Notes on Ingelburu Caves' below shows an example of this.

o Avoid crossing out every spelling mistake. The correct version could be written in the margin or underneath.

o Do not correct all the language and punctuation errors. Decide what is important in each piece of work.

o Write at the bottom any key words which were misspelt so that they can be written into a glossary and learned.

o Try to write a positive constructive comment such as 'Well done, I especially liked your vivid description'.

o Keep other comments constructive and upbeat, 'Next time think about…'.

o Depending on your school's marking policy, it is sometimes a relief to mark without giving a grade but just a written comment.

o Consider giving two marks, especially for creative projects: one, for academic content and the other, for overall 'artistic' presentation/originality. This is a useful way of acknowledging creativity and original thinking.

o Avoid red pen.

- - - - Notes on Ingelburu Caves - - - -

Ingelburu belonges to Regenald Fara. He = Botonist.
Lots of rodedendrens. There are tunnels in Nature trail.
Crippel hole/squeeze holes = grey rocks - gritstone (look like sheep)

Caves. Opened by James Farrer in 1837. We wereGiven Helmets. Caves = limestone only cos it is the only rock that can be disolved in water. Fell Beck made the cave, then fawnd a lower passsige. Made a wall of Tufa held back lake. They blowed it up. There was a micro invironment in the cave, where the lite had got to it. This ment that moss grew there. Tufa grew on moss. Calsite crystals were glinting

Elefants legs = piller

Copper = Tercoise

Algee = Tercoise

Ion = brown

Peet = brown

Disparity between content and spelling. Thanks to Neil Cottrell of LexAble Ltd for permission to use this illustration (his geography fieldwork notes, Year 6)

Organisation (see Chapter 9)

People with dyslexia often have very genuine problems with organisation. They are likely to misread instructions, get lost, forget equipment and arrive late and exhausted to lessons. Planning ahead and meeting deadlines can also cause difficulty and the student will need guidance.

Learning for tests and exams (see Chapter 10)

Students with dyslexia may have a poor short-term memory. They will need something to underpin the facts in order to get them into the long-term memory, so learning is going to take longer and will be harder than for most students.

Individual help

An *adult mentor* is a great help for students with dyslexia. Regular meetings with their mentor are useful to support the student, iron out difficulties as they arise, boost their confidence and celebrate successes.

A *specialist learning support teacher* can also provide invaluable academic support to a student with dyslexia.

Here are some personal or individual strategies for the students to try:

Reading

○ Students could use highlighters to emphasise key words when reading questions or instructions. This is very important in exams when nerves add to the likelihood of making dyslexic errors.

○ When reading it helps to use a ruler to keep the place. It is possible to get reading rulers, which have a small window slit to read through. This helps to prevent jumping lines.

○ Using coloured plastic overlays helps some students.

○ The background, colour and font size on a computer screen can be adjusted as necessary.

○ Students should read books with fast-moving stories, larger clear print, illustrations and not too much description. The publishers Barrington Stoke specialise in producing exciting stories for readers with dyslexia.

○ Listening to audio books of set texts will give students the overview. Students should also try to obtain a copy of the book, preferably with a larger print, to read as well.

o Text-to-speech software will read out the text and can make a huge difference. It is then possible for students to carry out the exercises that are required, having understood the passage or instructions.

Spelling

o Spelling rules should be learned.

o Phonetic sounds of letters and groups of letters should be revised.

o Students could make a glossary of key terms for each subject.

o Test key words regularly – reinforcement is important.

o Colour cards and drawings could be used to aid learning vocabulary.

o Make up mnemonics.

Revision techniques (see Chapter 10)

o Coloured card or sheets could be used so that the facts are related to a colour.

o Drawings, cartoons and funny stories could be used.

o The students could make up poems/songs/raps.

o Visual/kinaesthetic reinforcement should be used.

o Pictures, especially for learning vocabulary, could be used.

o Students could make voice recordings.

o Students could work with a friend and ask each other questions. They could teach some facts to each other.

o Mnemonics could be used both for tricky spellings and lists.

Order of planets in
_ _ _ _ _ distance from the Sun _ _ _ _ _

My Very Easy Method: Just Set Up Nine Planets
(Mercury, Venus, Earth, Mars, Jupiter,
Saturn, Uranus, Neptune, Pluto)

_ _

Avoid getting lost

Usually in secondary schools the teachers have set rooms and the students move from lesson to lesson. This can be very confusing for someone with dyslexia if they have a poor sense of direction. A plan of the school layout with lesson rooms marked will help, but the teacher also needs to check that they understand how to read the school timetable. Colour coding can often help, as can memorising left and right.

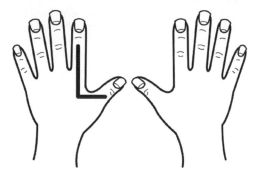

Figure 2.2 The left hand makes the letter L

Time keeping

Reading an analogue clock can be really difficult for some people with dyslexia, so they may genuinely not know the time. A digital watch is a good idea. Alarms can be set on digital watches to remind them when to set off for lessons (mobile phones also have alarms but some schools will not allow them).

Outside school, plans of routes or maps are useful in either paper or electronic form. The student will need to factor in time for getting lost until they are familiar with a route, and learn to arrive early or make a practice visit first to be sure of getting to the correct place on time, especially for important appointments. This is something I still do today!

Using specialist software for assistive technology

There is now a great range of assistive technology available for use by students with dyslexia and this can make a huge difference to their lives and academic achievement.

Using text to speech software has been the single most important coping strategy in my life.

Neil Cottrell was an intelligent student with severe dyslexia. He gained a first class honours degree in psychology and is now the director of an assistive software company LexAble Ltd

---

Students should take time to decide what their needs are and which devices or programmes will help them the most. The field is changing and developing very rapidly so it is worth seeking up-to-date advice. The British Dyslexia Association has a technology unit which gives advice and support (see page 222).

Some useful software includes:

- *Spell-checking programmes:* some work phonetically, while others have a playback facility. These can be excellent as they allow the student to concentrate on content rather than spelling.

- *Voice recognition software:* this can be brilliant for students with severe dyslexia as the software responds to the spoken word and will convert it into written text.

— *Text-to-speech software:* this reads text out loud and can be used with electronic text websites, emails, articles and scanned pages from books.

— *Scanners:* these convert pages into electronic format so that text-to-speech software can then be used. There are now scanners for books so that the text at the centre of the spine is not distorted.

– – –Key points – – – – – – – – – – – – – – – – –

★ Dyslexia is a problem with reading, writing and spelling.

★ It affects about 10 per cent of the population.

★ It is not linked to general overall intelligence.

★ Organisational skills can also be poor.

★ Students with dyslexia can learn coping strategies to work around their difficulties.

★ Multisensory teaching techniques are important.

★ Sensitive classroom teachers can make a huge difference.

Chapter 3
Dyscalculia

A word at the start

The aim of this chapter is to help subject teachers who may have number work, calculations or graphs as part of their syllabus. It is not for mathematics teachers. There are many excellent books for teaching maths, and some are listed at the end of this book (see page 223).

* What is dyscalculia?
* How can I spot a student with dyscalculia?
* Common indicators
* Common strengths
* How can I help in the classroom?
* Individual help
* Key points

What is dyscalculia?

Dyscalculia is like dyslexia but with numbers.

People with dyscalculia have *difficulty with counting and arithmetic* which is not in line with their overall intelligence level. Dyscalculia can be defined as 'a condition that affects the ability to acquire mathematical skills' (Department for Education and Skills 2001).

In England, dyscalculia became recognised as a separate Specific Learning Difficulty (SpLD) in 2004. It can be diagnosed with specialist diagnostic tests (British Dyslexia Association).

Where does the name come from?

Dys comes from the Greek word meaning *difficulty*.

Calculia comes from the Latin word meaning *to count*.

So dyscalculia means *difficulty with counting*.

Around 5 per cent of the population have dyscalculia on its own, but a greater number have it in combination with another SpLD (Butterworth 2003).

Dyscalculia is found equally in boys and girls. It often runs in families so it is thought to have a genetic component. It cannot be cured but, with effective teaching, students can master some numeracy skills and devise effective coping strategies to succeed in adult life.

How can I spot a student with dyscalculia?

Look out for the student who seems to be articulate and intelligent, who performs well verbally and in written assignments, but is surprisingly poor in tasks where numbers and calculations are involved. They might also be inaccurate with number recall, lack confidence in mathematics and try to avoid number work if possible.

Common indicators

DOWNSIDES

Most students with dyscalculia will only show some of the following indicators.

Numbers

- Lacks an intuitive grasp of numbers: does not automatically know which number is larger or smaller than another.
- Unable to recognise number patterns to tell how many items there are in a group (even if less than 10). Will need to count them individually.
- Trouble rounding numbers up or down.
- Difficulty estimating answers.
- Will often count on fingers.
- May confuse similar looking numbers such as 3 and 8 or 6 and 9.
- Reverses numbers, for example 350 for 305.
- Problems with zeros – can be out by multiples of 10.
- No confidence in mathematical answers.
- Extreme difficulty learning times tables.
- Cannot do mental arithmetic.

○ Problems remembering numerical facts.

○ Failure to see connections between known number relationships. For example, if 3 + 5 = 8, then 5 + 3 = 8 or 30 + 50 = 80.

○ Difficulty remembering mathematical procedures: may have to keep relearning them.

○ If a procedure has been learned it will be followed mechanically and without confidence or understanding.

○ Not sure whether a procedure will make the answer larger or smaller.

○ Difficulty grasping percentages, decimal points and fractions.

○ Not easily able to transfer skills or procedures learned in solving one set of problems to tackle different problems.

Understanding written questions

○ Inclined to panic and go blank with number questions, especially when under pressure.

○ Difficulty working out what a question is asking.

○ Misreads maths symbols in questions, such as ÷ and − , + and ×, < and >.

○ Misreads or misunderstands the words in questions.

○ Liable to guess wildly.

○ Confused by brackets.

Short-term memory problems (sequencing difficulties)

These cause difficulty remembering:

○ numbers to work on during calculations

- a series of processes or instructions
- number sequences such as phone numbers or security codes
- scores in games or moves when playing strategic games such as chess.

More complex mathematical procedures

Not surprisingly these cause more problems, especially if the basics are shaky. Students may struggle with:

- remembering the formulae to solve problems with area, volume, mass, speed, acceleration, density
- temperature conversions
- money, especially converting currencies
- percentage increase or decrease
- negative values
- equations, especially if they involve fractions
- statistics, mean, median, mode, standard deviation.

Graphical representation

- Problems understanding and interpreting graphs
- Knowing which way round the axes should be drawn
- Getting the scales to fit the paper
- Scales not consistent or inappropriate
- Points inaccurately plotted
- Lines inaccurately drawn
- Inaccurate readings.

Getting somewhere on time

Telling the time can be a genuine problem. Students may have difficulty reading an analogue clock or 24 hour clock, and reading and understanding timetables or maps with grid references. They may also get lost easily.

Emotional responses

Students with dyscalculia may find themselves embarrassed in class, afraid of being asked a question and shown up in front of their peers. They often panic under pressure and will come up with elaborate, avoidance tactics to bipass maths. Extreme cases can lead to anxiety and 'maths phobia'.

Organisational skills (see Chapter 9)

Some students may have problems with organisation. This is covered separately as it is a common difficulty with several of the SpLDs.

Be alert to dyscalculia – if you suspect that a student has dyscalculia ask the SENCO (special educational needs coordinator) if it is possible to arrange for the student to be professionally tested. This could make a big difference.

Common strengths

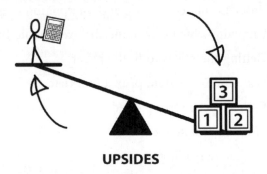

UPSIDES

A student with dyscalculia may be gifted in some of the following ways:

o Literate and expressive writer

o Poetic and artistic

o Good lateral thinker

o Intuitive

o Imaginative. artistic, creative, with a good sense of colour and texture

o Often good memory skills for language-based information

o Good verbally

o Empathetic and sensitive to others

o Outgoing and good at public speaking or acting

o Resourceful and tenacious

o Excellent team builder

o Good strategist.

- - - - - A view from the inside - - - - -

Professor Paul Moorcraft's book *It Just Doesn't Add Up* is a funny and uplifting story of his lifelong battle with dyscalculia and his success as an author, lecturer and war correspondent despite describing himself as number-blind.

He has invented the campaign slogan on behalf of all people with dyscalculia – JUST BECAUSE YOU CAN'T COUNT DOESN'T MEAN YOU DON'T COUNT.

- -

How can I help in the classroom?

Your attitude is important. Be sensitive, understanding and supportive and let any students with dyscalculia know that you are aware of their difficulties and you do not think they are stupid or lazy. This will make a big difference to their self-esteem.

Talk to the student about what works well for them and where they struggle. They may come up with several suggestions and it is good to listen. Be willing to try things out – you may need a more multisensory approach to get ideas across. Be relaxed and keep your sense of humour.

A few classroom practicalities

○ Make the classroom a safe, relaxed place where it is OK to make mistakes and to ask questions.

○ Do not cause embarrassment.

○ Keep students with dyscalculia near the front of the class. This helps engagement and also enables you to keep an eye on their progress.

○ Give short, clear instructions.

○ Give verbal as well as written instructions.

○ Repeat any key points.

○ Work through an example on the board, slowly and clearly.

○ Check regularly that everyone understands.

○ Give time for students to write down the example and explain exactly how you would like it to be laid out on the page.

○ If you have handed out printed sheets, read them out loud with the class and emphasise key points in a procedure.

○ Encourage students to read questions carefully and to take special notice of the symbols and key words. Suggest that they underline, use highlighters or vocalise them to themselves.

○ Leave enough time to go through the answers in class.

○ If a student has 'not got it' try to arrange a quiet time to go through it with them individually, maybe explaining in a different way.

○ If you want the whole class to work out a quick calculation, mini-whiteboards can be used and held up for you to see. These are fun and other students will not know who has got the right or wrong answer.

○ Do not ask a student with dyscalculia a sudden number question in class.

Mathematical language

○ Choose your language carefully. There are many words for the same mathematical processes and these can be confusing (see Figure 3.1).

○ Be consistent with your words.

○ Try to liaise with colleagues, especially those in the maths department. It increases confusion if teachers use different words for the same process.

- -

Science terminology can be even more confusing when terms are similar to everyday words. If students are imaginative they will visualise all sorts of things: science words such as pie charts, moles and webs conjure up food, furry animals and spiders.

Worse still, in the natural world, living cells multiply by dividing!

- -

ANSWER LARGER	+	X
> ↑	Plus Add Addition Sum of And How many altogether	Times Multiply Multiplication Sets or groups of product

ANSWER SMALLER	–	÷
< ↓	Minus Take away Subtract Subtraction Take ... from ... Difference between How much greater is --- than ---	Divide Division Share Share between How many ... in ... How many times can ... be taken away from ... How many times can ... go

Figure 3.1 Common mathematical processes

Writing on the board

- Make sure your handwriting is clear, or if you are using an electronic format, use a simple, large font.
- Space questions out well and separate them with a solid line.
- Give adequate time to copy. Remember there could be errors in the copying so be prepared to check.
- Give out printed sheets with important information on them. These must be stuck into their book immediately as unattached sheets get lost.

- Try changing the background colour for screen presentations and writing in colour.

Printed sheets

- Do not put too many examples on a sheet.
- Use a large, simple font.
- Leave white space. Crowded sheets are daunting and small print causes anxiety.
- Make handouts more fun with the odd cartoon.
- Lay examples out clearly. Show where an answer is to be written.
- Leave adequate space for working and to write the answer.
- Where appropriate, indicate the units to be used.
- Try using other paper colours rather than white. This might be clearer for some students. You could experiment with changing the writing colour too.

Counting

Students with dyscalculia are generally unable to estimate numbers quickly from a pattern and so they will have to count laboriously. Be aware that this will take much longer. Lack of confidence may also mean that they may recheck several times.

Fingers are really useful to count with, so let them know that this is fine. (Many adults with dyscalculia will still count on their fingers under the table due to embarrassment.)

Times tables

Some people with dyscalculia really struggle to learn and remember times tables, especially the more difficult ones such as 7, 8 or 9 times. Even if they are memorised for a test they are likely to be forgotten. It may help to let them have a times table square to refer to (see Figure 3.2). They could have their own to bring to the lesson or you could have some laminated to hand out.

x	1	2	3	4	5	6	7	8	9	10	11	12
1	1	2	3	4	5	6	7	8	9	10	11	12
2	2	4	6	8	10	12	14	16	18	20	22	24
3	3	6	9	12	15	18	21	24	27	30	33	36
4	4	8	12	16	20	24	28	32	36	40	44	48
5	5	10	15	20	25	30	35	40	45	50	55	60
6	6	12	18	24	30	36	42	48	54	60	66	72
7	7	14	21	28	35	42	49	56	63	70	77	84
8	8	16	24	32	40	48	56	64	72	80	88	96
9	9	18	27	36	45	54	63	72	81	90	99	108
10	10	20	30	40	50	60	70	80	90	100	110	120
11	11	22	33	44	55	66	77	88	99	110	121	132
12	12	24	36	48	60	72	84	96	108	120	132	144

Figure 3.2 A times table square

If the multiplication itself is not the main theme of your lesson, allow them to use a calculator and do not worry too much. Be aware that however hard they try, many students with dyscalculia will still be unlikely to memorise and retain their times tables.

A visual way to learn the 9x table

Fold down the finger of the number you want to multiply by

Count the rest of the fingers

The fingers to the left of the folded finger represent tens, and the
fingers to the right of the folded finger represent units

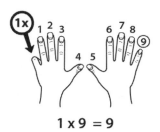

1 x 9 = 9

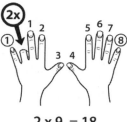

2 x 9 = 18

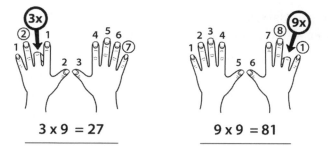

3 x 9 = 27

9 x 9 = 81

Figure 3.3 A handy way to remember the 9 times table

Untidy presentation

This will not apply to all students with dyscalculia but if it is
the case, the following ideas may help:

- Use paper with ruled squares. Try different sizes.
- Use large sheets of paper.

- Use worksheets with gaps to fill in, and limit the writing required.
- Encourage underlining headings.
- Rule off after each example. This is better if it is in pencil to avoid smudging ink.

Teaching formulae and rules

- If it is important, give students a printed copy.
- Use colour to reinforce learning.
- Drawings may help.
- Song, rap and rhythm can be useful to memorise rules.
- Use mnemonics.

Multisensory teaching

Try to make examples as multisensory as possible and related to real-life examples.

- Visual aids: posters, models and hands-on discovery. There are several suppliers of posters and models but, if time permits, let students make their own. This is fun, reinforces the learning point and can make an attractive classroom display.

- Use solid materials that students can see, touch and relate to. Sometimes the crazier the example, the better.

- There are some commercially available colourful and attractive mathematical materials such as Cuisenaire rods, Numicon, Stern materials and 3D teaching shapes from listed suppliers.

- Use everyday stuff, such as the following:
  - tape measures
  - metre rules

- rope/string
- children's building blocks
- plasticine or play-doh
- plastic bottles
- boxes, cereal packets
- coloured beads
- playing cards
- counters
- sweets.

o Rhythm and music are also great ways to remember facts.

o Computer programs: some good interactive programs are available.

Here are a just a few kinaesthetic multisensory examples:

o Volume can be demonstrated using different sizes and shapes of boxes, measuring cylinders or kitchen measuring jugs. Sand, grain or dried beans can be used to fill the space and then the volume measured. Coloured water can also be used if the containers are waterproof.

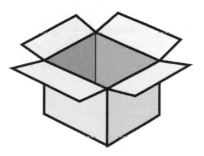

My biology class were intrigued to see the average daily urine output displayed as coloured yellow water in a series of 500cm^3 plastic drinks bottles - much easier to comprehend and remember than a figure in a book!

- ○ Surface area to volume ratios: use potatoes to make chips of the same length and thickness and then cut the chips into different numbers of blocks. This shows the same volume but differing surface areas – the smaller the pieces, the greater the overall surface area. Children's bricks can also be used, or card cut into pieces and drawn round.

- ○ Circles and pie charts: roll out balls of Play-Doh or plasticine into circles and cut out slices. Some cheeses are also circular, with individual sectors wrapped. This illustration could be even more memorable if cake is introduced one lesson!

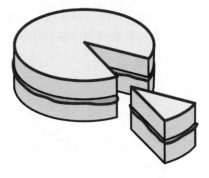

- ○ Percentages: use 100cm^3 measuring cylinders and coloured water filled to different levels.

- Movement, speed, acceleration: some children's toys can also be fun here, such as wooden toy trains for electric circuits; they can even carry different numbers of currants (pun intended, not a dyslexic error!).

- Balance: use see-saws (from a doll collection, or simply use a ruler balanced on a rubber). Metal coat hangers can be used to make a simple mobile.

Setting homework

- Remember, students with dyscalculia will be slower than their peers so decide which questions must be done and which should be tackled only if they have time.

- Be clear how much time you expect them to work for. Some students will struggle on for hours. Others will give up and not try.

- Give homework instructions early in the lesson.

- Write the homework on a board, or give out printed instructions and read aloud as well.

- Make sure that homework has been written down correctly and in a safe place, ideally a homework diary. You could ask them to read it back to you.

- If school allows, students could put the homework into their mobile phone 'notes'. This could even be dictated to avoid errors in writing.

- Find out if you can put homework on the school intranet.

- Do not set too many examples as this becomes daunting.

- Say exactly when and where homework is to be handed in.

Marking

- Try to mark frequently to make sure that the students are progressing well and understand.

- Be encouraging. If the method is correct but there is a mathematical error or transposed numbers, be positive and just point out where the error is. Try to give marks for method.

- Acknowledge progress and not only when they get everything right. Stickers or stars are usually popular.

- Avoid red pen and large red crosses. Green is preferable and somehow less threatening.

Individual help

Students with dyscalculia will benefit from individual specialist teacher support and extra time in examinations. A main part of the individual sessions will be to:

- reinforce lesson material
- give extended practice of methods
- build confidence with numbers
- develop a sense of number values
- gain an understanding that numbers can be manipulated and rounded up or down for easier calculation.

Ideally, a *learning support teacher* can work closely with the relevant subject departments to help with their curriculum needs.

Specialist teachers will generally come with an armoury of excellent ideas, but here are a few that sometimes help:

Reading accuracy

In order to avoid misreading symbols and words, encourage the student to highlight or underline the symbol or key phrase.

Some students like to talk to themselves to work out calculations; this can distract others, so encourage them to whisper or just mouth the words.

Short-term memory difficulties

Any methods that help to make facts 'stick' are useful. Use colour, drawings, mnemonics, catchphrases, rhythm or song. Lots of practice and reinforcement will be needed and it's important to revisit material frequently.

Number recognition (visualisation of number groups)

This is the ability to look at a random scatter of dots or objects and know how many there are without counting them individually. This skill relies on pattern recognition. Encourage playing card games and dominoes to see number patterns (see Figure 3.4).

Number patterns making 10

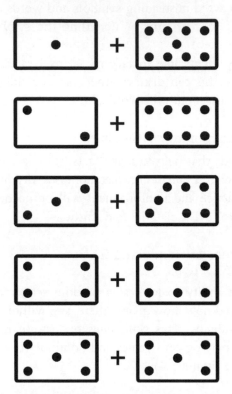

Figure 3.4 Some simple number patterns

Computer games

There are many interactive number games available, and students generally enjoy playing them. The difficulty levels can be graded so that they are non-judgemental and students can progress.

Visual problems

Some students may suffer from visual stress (see Chapter 2). This may cause difficulty with accurate work such as interpreting graphs or measuring.

Confidence

This is probably most important of all and it comes gradually and with success. There will be a noticeable reduction in anxiety if the student is given coping strategies to remember information, guidelines to follow and lots of practice.

A teacher who is approachable, fun, relaxed and adaptable can make all the difference.

- - - Key points - - - - - - - - - - - - - - -

* Dyscalculia is a recognised SpLD.

* It is a problem with numbers and arithmetic.

* It affects about 5 per cent of the population.

* Students with dyscalculia can learn to compensate for their difficulties.

* Multisensory teaching and solid, everyday examples are helpful.

* Sensitive classroom teachers can make a huge difference.

Chapter 4

Dysgraphia

* What is dysgraphia?
* How can I spot a student with dysgraphia?
* Common indicators
* Common strengths
* How can I help in the classroom?
* Individual help
* Key points

What is dysgraphia?

Dysgraphia is a lesser known Specific Learning Difficulty (SpLD) which affects *handwriting and converting thoughts to written words.*

People with dysgraphia are within the normal intelligence range but they struggle to put their ideas down clearly and coherently on paper. Their writing may be illegible or untidy despite considerable effort, and there is a disparity between ideas and understanding expressed verbally and those presented in writing. Their reading ability is normal and spelling may be affected, but this is not always the case.

Dysgraphia is thought to affect up to 10 per cent of the population to varying degrees (NHS Choices) and it can affect both boys and girls. It often occurs with other SpLDs but not always. There is a tendency for it to run in families.

The American Psychiatric Association (2013) describes dysgraphia as 'impairment in written expression' and 'writing skills (that)…are substantially below those expected given the person's…age, measured intelligence, and age-appropriate education'.

Where does the
name come from?

Dys comes from the Greek word meaning *difficulty*.

Graphia comes from the Greek word meaning *writing*.

So dysgraphia means *difficulty with handwriting*.

There are three forms of dysgraphia and the symptoms and effective treatment may vary depending on the cause.

○ *Spatial dysgraphia:* poor visual processing and understanding of space. This causes difficulty writing on lines and spacing letters. Drawing and colouring will also be affected. Both copied and original work is untidy and may be illegible. Spelling is normal

○ *Motor dysgraphia:* poor fine motor control of hand and wrist muscles, which makes writing difficult and tiring and generally results in untidy or illegible writing even when copying. Spelling is not affected

○ *Processing dysgraphia (sometimes called dyslexic dysgraphia):* difficulty visualising the appearance of the letters in a word, which results in the letters being malformed and in the wrong order when written. Original written work is illegible but copied work is fairly good. Spelling is poor.

Individuals may have one form of dysgraphia or a combination.

How can I spot a student with dysgraphia?

The student is probably bright and eloquent but consistently hands in work that looks untidy and is well below the quality that you would expect. If you watch them write, you may notice that the process can be laborious and their posture and pen grip look awkward. They are slow to copy from the board or from a book and they may complain of an aching hand.

Common indicators

DOWNSIDES

Spatial dysgraphia

- Not writing on the lines.
- Not able to follow margins.
- Problems organising words from left to right.
- Inconsistent space between words and letters; may be too close or too far apart.
- Irregular size, shape and slant of letters.
- Trouble reading maps or following directions.

- Difficulty drawing and colouring.
- Problems laying out arithmetic answers or doing geometry.

Motor dysgraphia

- Writing is very poor and difficult to read.
- Very slow writing, either original writing or copying from a board or book.
- Gets tired quickly when writing.
- May suffer from painful cramps while writing for extended periods.
- Abnormal pen grip and hand position.
- Unusual wrist, body or paper position.
- May struggle to use mathematical instruments.
- Difficulty drawing graphs.
- Other skills involving fine motor control affected such as doing up buttons or manipulating science apparatus.

Processing dysgraphia

- The physical act of writing takes a lot of concentration so they are unable to process information at the same time as writing.
- Difficulty remembering how to form some letters.
- Some letters are unfinished or backwards.
- Mixture of small and capital letters on the same line.
- Mixture of printing and cursive writing on the same line.

- Omitted letters or whole words, or repeated letters or words.
- Poor and erratic spelling and punctuation.
- May put in the wrong word in a sentence.
- Difficulty organising thoughts logically on paper; loses train of thought.
- Misses out key information.
- Writes long, rambling sentences with repetition.
- Very slow to think and compose sentences.
- Will underperform in tests and exams.

Other indicators

- Fluent when speaking but stilted language and limited ideas expressed on paper.
- May say the words out loud when writing.

Emotional responses

- May suffer from disappointment as written work takes a lot of effort and will always look poor.
- Written tasks can cause extreme frustration and stress.
- May fall behind academically as all written work takes much longer so they may not finish what is required in an allotted time.
- May try to avoid written tasks altogether or write as little as possible.
- Low self-esteem.

Common strengths

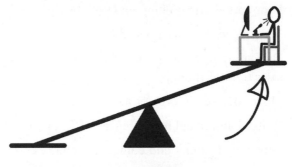

UPSIDES

○ Normal or high intelligence.

○ No social or behavioural difficulties.

○ Generally no other underlying academic problems.

○ May be very good orally and come up with interesting and unusual ideas.

○ Creative and imaginative, good in visual arts or design.

○ Computer-based skills often very good.

○ May be talented in music, drama, sport or other areas of the curriculum not requiring writing.

How can I help in the classroom?

Your attitude is important. Show that you understand that the student's problems are genuine and they are not being sloppy or lazy when written work looks untidy. Be sympathetic but also make it clear that you think they are intelligent and capable of achieving a high standard academically. Be aware that the act of writing needs extra concentration and so a student will not be able to understand and process information at the same time as writing.

Find ways to work around the student's difficulties to enable them to keep up with the rest of the class. Let them know that you are happy to help them on an individual basis should the need arise. It may be worth naming a time and place each week where you are available, if they wish to come and see you. Some teachers have a regular 'surgery' time when any students can come. Be positive and cheerful and try to boost their self-belief. Luckily nowadays there are ways to avoid too much handwriting.

During lessons

- Most importantly, reduce the amount of written work that is required – this will allow students with dysgraphia to keep up with the academic content of your subject.

- Give out printed notes so they have a correct and legible copy to learn from.

- If printed notes have gaps to fill in by hand, make sure that the spaces are large enough to accommodate larger or poorly positioned writing. Possibly increase the size and use double spacing, and print on bigger paper if necessary.

- Give out sets of short, closed questions to answer rather than instructions such as 'write a paragraph on'. This will guide the student's thinking and help them organise ideas into a logical sequence.

- Graph paper can be useful to help with the layout of mathematical calculations.

- Use paper with raised margins or lines to aid layout.

- Check that the student is keeping up with the pace of the class if writing is involved.

- Allow the use of a computer for longer pieces of work such as essays or projects and also for classwork, if this is possible. This will allow editing.

- Find out if students can sound-record part of the lesson.

- Encourage students to rub their hands together or shake their hands downwards periodically to relief tension and improve blood flow. Doing small push-ups from a sitting position can bring some relief.

- Allow extra time for written tests.

Sitting position

- Try to ensure that the student sits in an upright position with their feet on the ground (see Chapter 5, Figure 5.1).

- Make sure that they are not too close to other students as they may need elbow room.

- If the student sits near the front, you can keep an eye on their progress.

Homework

- Try to be imaginative and flexible.

- Students with dysgraphia write more slowly than others if they are writing by hand so they will not be able to produce as much homework in a set time.

- Allow the use of paper with larger line spaces or raised lines.

- Allow the use of technology if it is feasible – either a word processor or voice-assisted software.

- Is there another way that students can present their work? Perhaps they can make a PowerPoint presentation rather than an essay, or create a flow diagram, mind map, timeline or cartoon graphic. Would a voiceover, song or poem be appropriate?

For notes on organising thoughts on paper for essays and projects, see Chapter 9.

Marking

- o Mark for content not appearance.
- o Try to be encouraging and make constructive suggestions.
- o Acknowledge effort and improvement.
- o Avoid red pen.

Tests and exams (see Chapter 10)

- o Alternative ways of testing, such as oral tests, preparing a debate or giving a short presentation; multiple-choice questions can be very challenging and require less writing.
- o Special arrangements may be in place for public exams. Make sure that you are aware of these. Students could qualify for extra time or can use a word processor or voice recognition software. If this is the case they will need to practise this in school exams and tests.

Individual help

Students may benefit from individual help and advice from an *occupational therapist* or *specialist learning support teacher*. They can give helpful, practical advice and introduce the student to a range of products and strategies.

Exercises

- ○ Hand exercises can improve fine motor control.

- ○ Writing warm-up exercises may be helpful. Rubbing the hands together or shaking them can also relieve muscle tension.

- ○ Extra instruction and practice at writing. Some people with dysgraphia can develop a nice cursive writing style which they can use if they have to. It takes a lot of energy and concentration to write nicely and it is very slow, so would not be their chosen method but is useful at times.

- ○ Pen hold – very often people with dysgraphia have an incorrect pen grip or they grip too hard. Training may be needed to adapt to a more conventional grip such as the tripod grip shown in Figure 4.1.

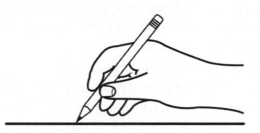

Figure 4.1 Tripod pencil hold

- ○ Special shaped pens or rubber pen grippers (see Figure 4.2) are available and some students find them helpful (see the Resources list on page 226).

Figure 4.2 Rubber pencil grip

Advice about seating position

It may be that students find it easier to use a writing slope which enables them to write with the paper placed at a slight angle. These are available commercially. A posture pack may also be beneficial. This is a wedge-shaped pillow that helps to maintain a good sitting position to aid writing.

Figure 4.3 Writing position using a writing slope

Vision

It is worth checking for visual tracking problems as it could be that the student's eyes are not working together properly. A specialist behavioural optometrist would advise and might suggest some form of vision therapy.

Use of technology

Using a computer for writing has benefited many students with dysgraphia. The student should be taught to touch type efficiently.

Voice recognition (or speech recognition) software can be obtained. It allows the student to talk to the computer, which will produce the words as text. There are a variety of products on the market. These have been shown to make a huge difference to students with dysgraphia who are then free to think clearly as they 'talk' their ideas to the software.

- - - Key points - - - - - - - - - - - - - - -

* Dysgraphia is a recognised SpLD.

* It is a problem with the physical act of handwriting and with organising thoughts on paper.

* Students have normal to above-average IQ and reading ability. Spelling may be affected but this is not always the case.

* Early diagnosis and writing therapy can help greatly but the problem will not be 'cured'.

* Teachers should be sympathetic and mark for content not appearance.

* Students will need extra time for handwritten assignments.

* The use of technology will transform the quality of work produced.

Chapter 5

Dyspraxia

* What is dyspraxia?

* How can I spot a student with dyspraxia?

* Common indicators

* Common strengths

* How can I help in the classroom?

* Outside the classroom

* Individual help

* Key points

What is dyspraxia?

People with dyspraxia have *difficulty with muscular coordination and movement.* The muscles themselves are normal but dyspraxia is the result of a 'brain-wiring' (neuro-biological) disorder. Fine motor skills which control precision movements, especially of the hands, or gross motor skills which control whole body movements can be affected, and so can speech.

Executive function skills are also affected by dyspraxia so this results in problems with organisation, short-term memory, planning and social interaction.

Motor coordination difficulties + organisation difficulties
= dyspraxia

Dyspraxia occurs on a continuum from mild to severe and it does not affect overall intelligence.

The cause of dyspraxia is unknown and there may be several contributory factors. In some cases there is evidence that it may run in families. It is thought that up to 5 per cent of children in the UK may have some degree of dyspraxia and it is currently diagnosed more often in boys than in girls (NHS Choices; Lingam *et al.* 2009).

Where does the name come from?

Dys comes from the Greek word meaning *difficulty*.

Praxia from the Greek word meaning *doing*.

So dyspraxia means *difficulty doing*.

Developmental coordination disorder (DCD) is another term used for dyspraxia, and the two terms are often used interchangeably. The term 'developmental' means that the person is born with the condition and it does not occur as a result of injury or illness. For simplicity, the term 'dyspraxia' will be used throughout this chapter.

- - - - · Definition of dyspraxia · - - - -

Developmental Coordination Disorder (DCD), also known as dyspraxia, is a common disorder affecting fine and/or gross motor coordination in children and adults (Movementmatters.uk).

The Dyspraxia Foundation adds to the Movement Matters description, recognising the many non-motor difficulties that may also be experienced by people with the condition and which can have a significant impact on daily life activities. These include memory, perception and processing as well as additional problems with planning, organising and carrying out movements in the right order in everyday situations. Dyspraxia can also affect articulation and speech (Dyspraxia Foundation, 2015).

- -

How can I spot a student with dyspraxia?

Look for the student who may arrive at your lesson flustered and slightly late. They might drop things, lose or forget equipment, fidget or even fall off the chair! They can contribute well in class but their written work is untidy and disorganised and doesn't seem to do justice to their ability. They might struggle with sport, especially ball games, and are frequently last to be picked for a team.

Common indicators

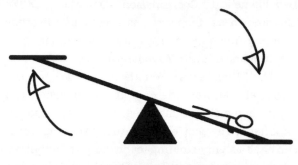

DOWNSIDES

Students with dyspraxia will show some of the indicators listed but not all of them. Remember that some students may also have other specific learning difficulties as well.

Gross motor skills

- ○ Poor coordination; may appear clumsy.
- ○ Liable to trip, spill or drop things.
- ○ May fidget in class.
- ○ Spatial awareness poor, liable to bump into people or objects.
- ○ Difficulty with games due to coordination problems. Poor at catching a ball, balancing, gymnastics, riding a bicycle, dance.
- ○ Untidy and scruffy appearance.

Fine motor skills

- ○ Poor handwriting and immature drawing skills.
- ○ Difficulty using instruments in subjects such as geometry, science, cookery and design technology.

○ Slow to dress – problems with buttons, ties and shoelaces.

Organisation

May have difficulty with the following:

○ Following timetables – may forget or muddle arrangements.

○ Time keeping – often arrives late and flustered.

○ Allocating time to tasks.

○ Finding the right way – goes to the wrong room or arrives at the wrong time. Poor sense of direction.

○ Keeping files, books and equipment in order.

○ Bringing correct equipment to lesson.

○ Remembering to do homework, does the wrong homework or does the homework but forgets to hand it in.

○ Keeping notes in order.

Poor short-term memory

May have difficulty with the following:

○ Remembering a set of instructions or a routine.

○ Recalling names of people and places.

○ Remembering codes, phone numbers or where lessons take place.

○ Retaining numbers while working out maths problems so may struggle with mental arithmetic but can be good at more difficult maths challenges.

○ Memorising times tables.

○ Revising quickly – it takes longer to learn because information must be stored in the long-term memory.

o Retaining information – must re-learn the material regularly.

Tests and exams

o Essay answers are disorganised as thoughts are disjointed.

o Mistiming exams – may spend too long on one question or attempt the wrong number of questions.

o Handwriting may be very poor; work looks scruffy and may deteriorate when time pressure and fatigue take over.

o Written work may include frequent crossing out.

o Difficulty interpreting questions – may take them too literally or not give enough detail in answers.

o Answers are often shorter than expected. This can be due to the act of writing being tiring or because the subtle inferences of the question are missed.

Sense perception

Students with dyspraxia may be over-sensitive to incoming stimuli (light, sound, touch, smell, taste) or they may be under-sensitive and this will affect their behaviour.

Over-sensitive:

o Dislikes the feel of certain fabrics or food textures or being touched by others.

o Background noise is difficult to filter out; may cover ears, hum, or tap a pencil to block out noise, especially if concentrating.

o Dislikes certain sounds.

o Suffers sensory overload with bright or flashing lights.

○ May find classrooms with displays and posters very distracting.

○ Some students cannot process information from more than one sense at a time so may look away if they are listening to cut out extra input. (This has unfortunate consequences as they may appear rude and miss out on body language clues.)

Under-sensitive:

○ May be less sensitive to the cold or to pain than most students.

○ May be rough with others in play.

○ Liable to fidget to get feedback for muscle receptors which will help maintain balance.

- -

Jane invariably walked around in shirt sleeves in winter despite pleas by her parents and school staff. She did not feel the cold.

- -

Social and emotional

○ May be less emotionally mature than peer group.

○ Poor interpersonal skills.

○ Difficulty reading body language.

○ Cannot easily pick up inferred or implied information.

○ Literal interpretation of language, so liable to miss jokes.

○ Unaware of the norms of personal distance; might stand too close or too far away from others.

- ° Does not 'fit in with the crowd'; often unable to participate in friendly chatter as they don't know what to say or their interests are different.

- ° Wants to have friends but unsure how to engage on a light, social level.

- ° Finds socialising tiring; may wish to have some quiet time alone.

- ° May become isolated and a 'loner'. This is increased by a poor ability at team sport which they will try to avoid.

- ° May develop compensatory mechanisms which can be inappropriate – interrupting conversations, being disruptive, or taking on the role of class 'joker/clown' to get a response. The peer group might find them immature and annoying.

- ° Some students will compensate by immersing themselves in computer games or books to avoid social contact and possible rejection.

- -

Emilie was never without a book, even at meal times. She always had the next book with her when halfway through her current one. This was to ensure that she was never without. She found the company of fictional characters much less tiring.

- -

Depression

This is a common problem for students with dyspraxia. It can result from:

- ° feeling clumsy and awkward

- ° embarrassment and possible physical pain when accidents occur o not being able to excel in school sports

o written work looking scruffy and receiving negative feedback from teachers

o not feeling valued for their real intellect or potential

o low self-esteem

o friendship issues

o being vulnerable – may be bullied and the butt of jokes as they are seen to be different and socially awkward

o becoming socially isolated.

Tiredness

A lot of extra effort has to go into performing physical actions, remembering things and dealing with social encounters. The result is that students with dyspraxia often get very tired coping with a school day. They really value some quiet time if it is possible.

- -

> Imagine riding a bicycle with loose handlebars. To ride it you would need to be constantly correcting the steering as every bump sends the front wheel off course. You could never relax and it would be very tiring. This is what dyspraxia is like for me. Simple actions sometimes need an inordinate amount of concentration and it is hard not to feel a degree of inadequacy when others can be seen to accomplish these tasks so effortlessly.
>
> *John, student with dyspraxia*

- -

Common strengths

UPSIDES

- Lateral, imaginative, 'outside the box' thinker.
- Creative; may shine at design, use of colour and textures, photography.
- Able to recall events from long ago in detail.
- May have a special interest in certain topics and be very knowledgeable about them.
- Imaginative; good at writing, stories, plays or poems.
- May excel at maths.
- Good at literature or poetry.
- ICT skills may be very good.
- Determined and will persevere along a chosen path. Life has always presented obstacles, therefore they are not easily deterred.
- May be good orally and do well in debating, telling stories or acting.

- o Good with younger children or animals.
- o Refreshingly honest.

- - - - - **A view from the inside** - - - - -

Lying diagonally in a parallel universe means that we have a brilliant and unusual slant on life. We see things that others can't, and for this reason I feel that we are very lucky to be dyspraxic.

From her book Caged in Chaos: A Dyspraxic Guide to Breaking Free. *A funny but poignant autobiography describing her time at a British boarding school*

- -

How can I help in the classroom?

Just by being aware of the student's genuine difficulties you will already have made a difference. Students with dyspraxia often feel 'clumsy and stupid', so it is important to let them know that you do not think of them as either.

Be clear that you value their intellect and contributions to the class and you do expect them to do well.

Work with them and discuss what techniques help them to learn the best. Be open to ideas from the students. They are the experts in dealing with dyspraxia and they can help you come up with effective strategies.

Motor difficulties

- o Seating: are the seats in your classroom easy to balance on? Science labs are often the worst as students can be expected to balance on high stools. Is there an alternative? Ideally the student should be sitting with their back supported upright and with their feet placed firmly on the ground.

When you are perching on a high stool with no back or arms, you may be so busy trying to keep your balance that you can't listen to the teacher.

Victoria Biggs, from her book Caged in Chaos: A Dyspraxic Guide to Breaking Free

---

- Let students with dyspraxia sit near the front. This means that they can see the board clearly and you can observe their progress. They can feel more involved in the lesson and are less likely to get distracted. They are also better sitting at the end of a row rather than in the middle.

- Fidgeting: if they are jiggling it can be to maintain balance and get muscle feedback. Try not to get irritated. They may benefit from moving around the room periodically.

- Something to fiddle with: a stress ball or equivalent can be useful and it sometimes aids concentration. It might also stop them from tapping with a pencil, which annoys everyone.

- Anticipate potential accidents: make sure the students are aware of steps or other obstacles near your classroom.

- Keep classroom floor clear of clutter: school bags, books or coats on the floor are trip hazards. Particular care will be needed for practical subjects.

- If you teach a practical subject accidents will happen! Try to keep calm and be aware of the procedure if equipment is broken or solutions are spilt. Just try to keep the student as safe as possible.

○ Using equipment: fine motor control difficulties can make it hard to use instruments requiring dexterity. Try to anticipate problems and avoid embarrassment. Special equipment can be provided if the school budget allows. Larger or Easi-Grip® scissors, more stable containers or adapted geometry instruments could make life easier.

Giving notes (see Chapter 2)

○ Reduce the quantity of handwriting required as much as possible. Give out printed notes possibly with gaps to fill in so the student can keep up with the lesson and stay engaged.

○ Physically writing notes will be exhausting and the result could be inaccurate and illegible.

○ Short-term memory problems may cause difficulty.

I could never copy from the board. By the time I had looked down I had forgotten what I was supposed to be writing down.

John, student with dyspraxia

○ If the student is concentrating on their handwriting they will not be able to process or remember the content.

Writing and presentation (see Chapter 4)

○ This will often be slow, laborious, inaccurate and untidy. Pens and pencils with different grips, non-slip rulers and other adapted mathematical instruments can be purchased.

○ Writing position: try to make sure that the students are sitting square to the table with their feet firmly on the floor, weight even. The table should be at a comfortable height (see Figure 5.1).

○ A writing slope or seat wedge might also help (see Chapter 4, Figure 4.3).

Figure 5.1 An ideal sitting position

○ Using large paper or squared paper can help with layout.

○ Check the student's written work regularly for accuracy.

○ Students should continue to practise handwriting and fine motor skills even though it is difficult.

Multisensory teaching (see Chapter 2)

○ Try to reinforce your lessons in a multisensory way. Include visual, audio and kinaesthetic input and vary the activities.

○ Lessons are more memorable if active participation is involved.

○ Reducing the time spent writing allows students more time participating.

Use of computers and assistive technology

- Students with dyspraxia should be encouraged to practise their computer skills as often as possible, especially with essays and projects.

- Using a keyboard removes the physical difficulty of writing and students can then concentrate on the content of what they are writing and on their flow of thoughts. Often the result is much more mature and insightful.

- Paragraphs can also be moved about electronically and this helps with essay organisation.

- Work can be nicely illustrated and graphs and diagrams can be included.

- Some students prefer to take notes in class using a small word processor and it may be possible to provide such a device. Downloading and storing the information can be a problem, though, so this needs careful thought. Your school may have a policy on this.

- Recording devices such as voice recognition software can also be considered.

- The quality of the work produced using technology is a better reflection of the student's ability and can be something to be proud of.

Working with others

Working in pairs often works better if you choose pairs with complementary skills. They can divide the tasks, but make sure that both students are actively involved.

Group work can be challenging for students with dyspraxia but it can work well with a little 'stage management'. You should pick the groups to balance talents. This also removes any embarrassment about not being chosen. Students with dyspraxia may be seen as 'a bit odd' and they may not be selected by their peers. Ascribe different roles within the groups and watch out for unkindness or bullying. Change the groupings in different lessons.

Sometimes students with dyspraxia have their own very creative and different ideas and enjoy an opportunity to work alone and follow their own interests. I feel that this is OK on occasion, but not as the norm, and it is better if some others also wish to go solo.

Organisational skills (see Chapter 9)

Disorganisation is an integral part of being dyspraxic and this can seriously affect progress at school. Strategies for compensating and finding coping mechanisms are covered in Chapter 9.

HOMEWORK

- ○ Give this out early in the lesson.

- ○ Be very clear; it's best to give written instructions as well as verbal.

- ○ Could they dictate the homework into a mobile phone?

- ○ Does the school have an intranet system where homework is placed?

- ○ If you give out a printed sheet, make sure that it is fixed into their homework book You can print on sticky labels for instant fixing.

- ○ If students have copied homework down, check that it is correct.

- ○ Give clear instructions, including the time you would expect them to spend on the work, when it should be completed, where it should be handed in and if it can it be done on a computer.

- Show clearly how you would like a piece of work laid out. Instructions such as 'underline with a ruler', 'this diagram should fill half a page', 'draw a ruled box in pencil around a table' are helpful.

- Consider giving a larger version of a question sheet, especially if it has gaps to fill in or space for working. Do not be tempted to give out reduced-size question sheets in order to save paper.

- Could the student have a homework buddy who they can phone in the evening if they are unsure what to do?

- Set different types of homework from time to time such as creative projects, flow diagrams, mind maps, quizzes, word games, inventing songs, raps, poems, debates and games.

MARKING HOMEWORK

- Mark for content not presentation.

- Be encouraging, acknowledge and praise progress and effort.

- Try to give a useful and constructive comment for the student to think about next time.

- Decide what is important to correct this time.

- Avoid red pen.

Your support is valued by students with dyspraxia. Try to be consistent, approachable and open to ideas. Let the student know that you understand their dyspraxia and genuinely want to help make life easier. Celebrate successes when they occur and you will have already gone a long way to making a big difference.

Outside the classroom

There will be many other difficulties facing students with dyspraxia around school. It is useful to be aware of these even if they might not be directly relevant to your subject.

Games lessons

These can be a nightmare for students with dyspraxia for several reasons.

Changing takes much longer and may be upsetting, especially if the changing room is crowded: finding kit from bags or lockers, opening lockers with keys or codes, fumbling with buttons and shoelaces with time pressure and poor dexterity can all be very difficult and stressful.

- -

> To imagine what it feels like, put on large rubber gloves and try changing from a button shirt and smart trousers or skirt into games kit with lace-up trainers. Allow a five-minute time limit.
>
> *A student's description*

- -

○ Could the student go a little early to get changed at the beginning and end of games? This has the advantage that the changing room is not crowded, which reduces the chance of kit getting lost. It reduces stress and means that they are not in trouble for being late for the next lesson.

○ All kit should be clearly marked, preferably in large clear letters or with colour coding so it can be found quickly.

○ Parents could be encouraged to provide clothes that are easier to put on such as having Velcro® on shoes or shirts rather than laces or buttons.

- ° Spare PE equipment such as a school hockey stick or shin pads which can be borrowed can reduce stress when equipment is forgotten.

- ° Sometimes students' parents are happy to provide some spare games clothes, fully named, to be kept in the PE department for emergencies.

Team games are often genuinely difficult, especially if they involve throwing and catching a ball:

- ° The student will be conscious of letting others down.

- ° They are likely to be the last to be picked by peers so try to avoid this situation. It is usually easier if the teacher has already chosen teams in advance.

- ° Alternatively, can they help at sports fixtures as a scorer, line judge or time keeper? Being an official gives them a genuine sports role and they can travel to fixtures as a valued member of the team.

- ° As the student gets older they may wish to pursue other sports which are more suited to their skills. Swimming, line dancing, running, martial arts, pilates and kayaking have been recommended. These will help develop strength, improve coordination and increase confidence.

I have happy memories of taking a group of students for a weekly sailing lesson. The group included Olivia, who was an outgoing girl with dyspraxia, and her best friend Annie, who was an excellent sailor and more serious. Annie's skill and Olivia's enthusiasm and sense of fun made them a great partnership. A good time was had by all but we did have to allow an extra 15 minutes at the end to extricate Olivia from her wetsuit!

Author

Lunch and break time

- Lunch queues are busy and often stressful times. Carrying trays of food can be very perilous for students with dyspraxia. Could they have a buddy to carry the tray? Nothing is more embarrassing in a crowded dining room than dropping a full tray of lunch!

- They may eat lunch more slowly and more messily than their peers. If they are not too embarrassed to use a napkin it can save them from having a shirt with food stains for the afternoon.

- Can they go in to lunch a little early, with a friend?

- Is a packed lunch an option?

- Lunch and break times are unstructured and often unsupervised. They can be unhappy and stressful for students with dyspraxia as teasing and bullying can occur. The student may not want to join in with team games and prefer to pursue other interests. Sometimes other clubs or societies are a way of 'escaping'.

- -

At secondary school my son took refuge in the library at lunch time. He had a laptop but there was nowhere to plug it in or print out his work. The lockers were in a part of the building miles away from where he spent most of the day so he was always losing stuff or getting it pilfered.

Mother of boy with dyspraxia

- -

Social inclusion

Social situations can be challenging for students with dyspraxia and they can become isolated and depressed. Try to assure them that there are many options and valuable roles for them to fill.

○ Encourage them to go to interest clubs and activities within school. It is much easier to make friends through a common activity. There are many possibilities such as photography, film, chess, debating, politics, green issues, computer clubs and helping with junior societies.

○ Could they be a photographer or reporter for the school journal?

○ School drama or music productions offer a variety of roles, either on stage or behind the scenes. Being part of a production gives a sense of unity and a common purpose and creates a social network.

○ Involvement in charity work, either fundraising or community action, can be fun.

Individual help

A *designated adult mentor*, who sees the student individually on a regular basis, can make a big difference. The mentor can provide support for the student, deal with problems as they arise and help to increase their self-confidence by praising their achievements and progress. Often a mentor can act as a 'go-between', relaying the student's worries to their class teachers and vice versa.

A *specialist learning support teacher* is also very useful in providing tailored academic support for the student and advice for teachers.

There are other areas of extra support:

Coordination

○ Regular physiotherapy sessions to improve coordination skills.

- ○ Individual sessions in PE to practise skills such as ball handling and balance.

- ○ Dance lessons or martial arts.

- ○ Practising handwriting skills, drawing and fine motor control.

Social skills

It is helpful to reinforce topics covered in PSHE (personal, social and health education) lessons and to talk about areas which can cause difficulty or embarrassment:

- ○ How to engage in conversation.

- ○ How to interpret body language.

- ○ Inference and implied meaning.

- ○ Personal hygiene.

Organisation and time planning (see Chapter 9)

A mentor can help students to find coping strategies that work best for them. They will need continued support throughout school, including the sixth form.

Students may need additional help organising their school lives as new challenges come along. Help with time management skills such as how to set work priorities and meet deadlines, would also be useful.

Advice on essay and project planning can be found in Chapter 9.

Exams and revision (see Chapter 10)

Students who have dyspraxia may qualify for special arrangements in public exams. These could include extra time, using a word processor or having a scribe to write for them. They will need to be tested by a specialist assessor, and the school SENCO (special educational needs coordinator) and exams officer are responsible for ensuring that the necessary arrangements are in place. Students should also have these arrangements in school exams and tests to practise taking exams with the special arrangements in place.

Key points

* Dyspraxia is a recognised SpLD.

* It is a condition that causes problems with movement and coordination.

* Short-term memory, perception and social interaction can also be affected.

* Dyspraxia affects around 5 per cent of the population and is more often diagnosed in boys.

* Students with dyspraxia have many talents and skills but may be socially isolated.

* Friendships occur most easily if there is a common interest.

* Students benefit from using a computer or voice recognition software for written work.

* Supportive teachers can make a big difference.

Chapter 6

Attention Deficit Hyperactivity Disorder (ADHD)

* What is ADHD?
* How can I spot a student with ADHD?
* Common indicators
* Common strengths
* Whole-school policy
* How can I help in the classroom?
* Outside the classroom
* How is ADHD treated?
* Individual help
* Key points

What is ADHD?

People with ADHD often show three behavioural indicators: *inattention, hyperactivity* and *impulsiveness.*

ADHD is a neurobiological disorder (brain chemistry). It cannot be cured but it can respond to medicine, behavioural therapy and lifestyle changes. It is thought to affect up to 5 per cent of children and young people and is the most common behavioural disorder in the UK (NHS Choices). The severity varies over a continuum from mild to severe.

ADHD often runs in families, suggesting that there is a genetic link, but it can also be affected by environmental and lifestyle factors. It does not affect the overall intellect of the individual although it can impair their progress unless carefully controlled.

Many people with ADHD also suffer from other Specific Learning Difficulties (SpLDs) such as dyslexia or an autism spectrum disorder (ASD). They may also have additional problems such as insomnia and anxiety.

It has taken a long time for ADHD to be formally recognised as a genuine medical condition and not just the result of poor parenting, but it is now accepted by the World Health Organization.

Where does the name come from?

The American Psychiatric Association adopted the name 'attention deficit hyperactivity disorder' (ADHD) in 1994 in its *Diagnostic and Statistical Manual*. This name is now generally used and has largely replaced the British term 'hyperkinetic disorder'.

According to the American Psychiatric Association (2013), ADHD is 'a persistent pattern of inattention and/or hyperactivity-impulsivity that interferes with development, has symptoms presenting in two or more settings (e.g. at home and school), and negatively impacts directly on social, academic or occupational functioning. The symptoms must be present before age 12.'

There are three types of ADHD with differing symptoms:

o *Predominantly inattentive ADHD* – diagnosed more frequently in girls

o *Combined ADHD* – most common – inattentive and hyperactive/impulsive – diagnosed more commonly in boys

o *Predominantly hyperactive impulsive ADHD* – rare.

The old term *attention deficit disorder (ADD)* has now been replaced with *predominantly inattentive ADHD*.

- - - Brain chemistry and ADHD - - -

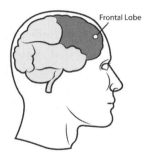

Frontal Lobe

The front part of the brain (frontal lobes) controls our rational and logical behaviour. It enables us to think before we act and to learn from experience. It also allows us to inhibit certain emotional responses, to modify our behaviour and to prevent us from taking risks that are unwise. The lobes are also the site of our personality, goal setting, planning and making us who we are.

Brain cells communicate using chemicals called neurotransmitters. It has been shown that people with ADHD have less neurotransmitter activity than usual in the frontal lobe region. This produces more risk taking, spontaneity and a lack of concentration.

How can I spot a student with ADHD?

It is easier to spot students who display hyperactivity and impulsiveness. They are probably the ones who cannot sit still, call out in class and are constantly demanding your attention. They can be bright, sparky and innovative but always seem to be attention seeking and need frequent disciplining. They could act as the class jester if bored, but they can also become angry or upset and erupt into an emotional outburst of temper.

The inattentive form of ADHD is much harder to detect. Students may appear to be rather dreamy and do not listen properly when you talk to them. They are disorganised and do not seem to take information in very well. They may avoid hard tasks and feel that they cannot cope.

Students with all types ADHD often really want to do well and please the teacher but they struggle with organisation and 'getting things right'. Their written work can be inadequate or incomplete, although they may have started out with great ideas. They may frequently argue and fall out with their peers, but this can sometimes be due to provocation and teasing.

Depression is a common problem among these young people, as they feel that they will never be able to keep friends and do well at school.

Common indicators

DOWNSIDES

Inattention

- ○ Easily distracted.
- ○ Short attention span; moves from one task to another.
- ○ Problems remaining focused on an activity.
- ○ May not listen properly.
- ○ Makes careless mistakes.
- ○ Lack of organisation – loses things, arrives late, forgets to hand in work.
- ○ Poor short-term memory.
- ○ Difficulty following instructions.
- ○ Appears rather detached and absent-minded.
- ○ Avoids tasks needing sustained mental effort.
- ○ Fails to complete tasks despite good intentions.

Hyperactivity

- ○ Fidgets with hands and jiggles legs when sitting. Appears restless and distracted.
- ○ Gets out of seat frequently in class.
- ○ Can be silly and show off.
- ○ Will run or climb at inappropriate times (in older children this can be replaced by a general restlessness).
- ○ Talks excessively.
- ○ Unable to relax and be calm.
- ○ Chaotic manner; arrives late without the correct books or equipment.

Impulsiveness

- ○ Shouts out in class.
- ○ Impatient.

- Excitable.
- Finds it difficult to wait for a turn.
- Interrupts and intrudes on other people's conversations.
- Can be anxious and agitated.
- Reacts emotionally, not rationally.
- Can become angry and aggressive.
- Risk taker; defiant.
- Always looking for the most exciting thing to do.

Executive function difficulties

Executive function skills enable us to organise and plan activities, to think logically and to carry out tasks successfully to completion. These functions work together to help us to reach personal goals, learn from mistakes and override impulsive behaviour.

Students with ADHD often struggle to develop these skills and so they may have difficulty with the following activities at school:

- Remembering details or instructions, and retaining numbers long enough to carry out a calculation.
- Focusing and sustaining attention.
- Organising, planning and prioritising.
- Estimating how much time a project will take to complete.
- Learning from experience and reflecting with hindsight.
- Regulating behaviour by thinking about consequences.
- Making rational decisions.
- Completing tasks – they often have great ideas, but are unable to persevere and complete them.

- Reacting logically rather than emotionally. This can cause issues with friendships and relations with teachers.
- Inhibiting certain impulsive behaviour patterns.
- 'Diffusing' build-up of emotion, resulting in temper outbreaks.

Common strengths

UPSIDES

- Great enthusiasm.
- Innovative ideas.
- Lots of energy.
- Different perspective as lateral thinker.
- Charismatic and engaging.
- Fearless. Will delight in trying new things; loves 'having a go'.
- Will volunteer readily.
- Can be excellent at acting, dance or sport.
- Often kind, friendly and outgoing.

- ○ Can be very good with younger children.
- ○ May rise to a challenge if given some responsibility.
- ○ Generally wants to do well and have friends.
- ○ May have a strong sense of justice and fairness.
- ○ May have a passion for a particular topic, sport or hobby.

Whole-school policy

Teachers should all be aware of any students with ADHD, and the SENCO (special educational needs coordinator) should give advice about their individual needs and strengths.

An *adult mentor* can really help a student with ADHD. Ideally they would meet the student every day and help them to cope with the challenges of daily school life. It is important that the mentor knows the student well and can relate to them in a positive and cheerful way but can be firm when necessary. Ideally the mentor should be accessible if needed during the day, both by the student and by teachers. The mentor can be a useful go-between between teaching staff and the student. This is especially valuable when there are misunderstandings. A free flow of information is essential.

Teaching assistants may be able to help in some lessons, which can be very beneficial to the student with ADHD, the teacher and to the others in the class.

Make sure that you are clear about the school policy and procedures and you know who the student's mentor is. Find out about the following:

Work matters

- ○ Does the student have any other learning difficulties?
- ○ Do they qualify for extra time or rest breaks in tests and exams?

- ○ Can they use a computer for assignments and exams rather than having to hand write?
- ○ Are there any special arrangements regarding homework?
- ○ Do they have individual learning support lessons?

Medical matters

- ○ Are they taking medication and how might this affect them?
- ○ Does the medication last all day? Some older students may take it selectively so that it is most effective for the lessons requiring greatest concentration.

If there are serious behavioural problems

- ○ Who should be contacted?
- ○ Is there a specified place that the student could go to if they have to leave your lesson?
- ○ Is there a colleague in a nearby room who can help you either with the student or the rest of the class if the student becomes disruptive or violent?
- ○ What is the school's policy on restraint?

Social matters

- ○ How often do they report to their mentor?
- ○ How can you contact the mentor to learn more or to pass on information?
- ○ If the student is being bullied in any way, what is the school policy on bullying?

Consistency across all staff about excepted norms of behaviour is important and will make it much easier for students and staff to work together.

How can I help in the classroom?

Your attitude is important. These students may be very trying at times. They are disorganised and may be behind with their work or they have mislaid it completely. In class they might shout out, have difficulty keeping quiet, leap out of their seat and disrupt lessons by demanding attention. However, they can also have exciting and interesting ideas, lots of enthusiasm and an unusual and original approach. This makes them both challenging and rewarding to teach.

If they have the inattentive form of ADHD they will be less disruptive but they can appear to be rude, disinterested and not listening to you. It is important that you try to keep them engaged and motivated and don't take it personally.

Remember that most students with ADHD would like to do well and they are sad and upset when things go wrong and their behaviour lets them down. You can help them a great deal by showing understanding and being positive and proactive in your approach.

- Let them know that you believe in them and in their ability.
- Have clear and fair discipline rules.
- Be approachable but firm.
- Be consistent in your behaviour and demeanour.
- Let them know that they can come and seek individual help from you.
- Remain upbeat and cheerful.
- Show that you care and remember to smile.

Planning lessons

- Always start the lessons the same way: this provides structure and security.

- Outline the aim of the lesson and the way it will take shape.

- Give information in short chunks.

- Keep instructions short and clear.

- Indicate the way that the time will be divided up during the lesson.

- Provide a checklist so the student can tick off tasks as they are completed and see how many tasks are left.

- Give frequent indications of remaining time – use statements such as, 'in five minutes we will move on'.

- Use a multisensory approach to keep interest levels up and use a variety of learning channels.

- Change the activity frequently and keep up the pace.

- Make the material as relevant as possible to real-life issues.

- Come up with innovative ways for them to record information – can they draw it, produce a cartoon strip, fill in boxes in text, do a computer flow diagram or make a computer graphic?

- Allow the use of coloured pens, highlighters and coloured paper.

- Be flexible on occasions and respond to the mood in the classroom. You may feel that you need to switch activity sooner than planned to keep the class focused or, if everyone is engaged in an activity, you may wish to let it run for an extra few minutes. Your agenda is a guide but is not 'carved in stone'.

Seating

A traditional seating plan works better with students sitting in rows facing the front. This is much less distracting than having them sitting in groups facing each other.

Figure 6.1 Seating arrangements

○ Students with ADHD should ideally sit at the front of the class or at the end of a row where you can walk past.

○ It is important to be able to have clear eye contact.

○ Let the student keep the same position for a term if it works well. This gives stability.

○ They should sit away from distractions such as a window, door, noisy pipes, wall displays or the class gerbil!

○ Sit them beside a sensible 'buddy' or a good role model.

○ Find an area at the back, perhaps a computer station or a more secluded corner where the student could go if they need a change of activity.

○ Is there an area where they can change their seating position to work? Sitting on a bean bag or lying on a mat to read might provide the change they need.

Discipline

- Be very clear with the whole class about expected norms of behaviour, both commendable and unacceptable.

- Outline exactly what is not acceptable and any consequences for misdemeanours.

- Be consistent about your class rules.

- Develop a signal to attract the student's attention if it has wandered; this can be more subtle and less embarrassing than using their name.

- Signal clearly if you feel that their behaviour is becoming unacceptable.

- Give them one warning and remind them of the consequences.

- If unacceptable behaviour continues act quickly, decisively and confidently to discipline the student.

- Do not lose your temper, try to remain calm and emotionally equable.

- Choose sensible punishments for misdemeanours, ones that you can actually carry out and that ideally 'fit the crime' as these are easier to relate to; for example, lateness or wasting lesson time can result in staying behind for five minutes at the end. (This will not always be feasible as it depends when the lesson falls, but the student can see it is fair.)

- Try to avoid direct confrontational arguments with the student, especially in front of the class.

- Learn to recognise the signs that the student is becoming stressed, anxious or angry in order to divert a difficult situation in some way. Can you change their activity or position in the classroom, send them on an errand or give them a task in the room? Can they go to a quiet area in the classroom?

○ If you feel that it is best if they leave the lesson, is there a designated place elsewhere in the school that they can go to relax and calm down? They will probably need to be accompanied.

○ Try not to bear a grudge even if the student has been rude to you. Deal with discipline calmly and firmly but try not to take it personally. It is part of their condition and they cannot always help it.

Allowing movement during the lesson

Some students will have a constant need to fiddle or jiggle. It is an idea sometimes to let them have a stress ball or piece of fabric to fiddle with. This can aid concentration and avoids them pencil tapping, which annoys others.

Try to factor in a time when the whole class can leave their seats and move around – for example, doing group work, acting out a scenario, having a debate, carrying out a practical exercise or going to look at a demonstration.

Allow a hyperactive student with ADHD to give out textbooks or paper or give back homework so that they have an excuse to move. They are likely to volunteer if you need an assistant for a task, but you have to try to balance the needs of others in the class too.

Use of computers

Working on computers can be very rewarding for students with ADHD and they often enjoy computer-based tasks. They are able to organise written work better, as paragraphs can be moved and words adjusted without making the presentation untidy. A piece of work can also be produced and illustrated to a high standard using a computer. This can be shown to the class using audio visual equipment, which is good for self-esteem. Work done on computers can be emailed to the teacher and is less likely to get lost.

Interactive teaching programmes are often very popular, especially if they are colourful and fun. They can give instant, non-judgemental and personal feedback, which is excellent for students with ADHD.

Team/pair work

- This is easiest if *you* choose the groups or pairs.

- Give specific roles to everyone in the groups as this avoids conflict.

- Divide the task into a series of small, achievable goals.

- Give a clear timescale to work to and remind the students, at an appropriate moment, how long they have left.

- Students with ADHD may have great ideas, but make sure their projects are realistic and achievable.

- Watch carefully for arguments or bullying.

Positive feedback, celebrating success

- Try to look out for good behaviour or work to celebrate during the lessons.

- Give immediate praise.

- Reward in a tangible way, such as a giving a sticker or house point, depending on the school system, or invent your own reward scheme. Be consistent though, and remember that there are others in the class.

- Acknowledge improvement and effort.

- Let the student's mentor or year head know about any successes so that they can give praise and positive feedback to the student and pass on this information to the child's parents. Often we only remember to pass on negative information, and these students need a morale boost.

Manage change carefully

Students with ADHD dislike changes in routine as this throws them into chaos. If you know that there will be a disruption in your class such as a visitor, cover teacher or a fire drill, try to let the class know beforehand. This will take away the surprise element and the student is less likely to overreact.

Responsibility in class

Students with ADHD may lack confidence and this can sometimes be helped by giving them a role of responsibility. Could there be a responsible role in some of your lessons? Is there a club or society attached to your subject that the student can help with? They are sometimes especially good with younger children, and having a responsible role can help with morale.

Organisation (see Chapter 9)

This is an area where students with ADHD will need continued support throughout school as they struggle with planning and meeting deadlines. Individual guidance will be needed to help them develop coping strategies.

Homework

○ Be aware that a piece of work will take a student with ADHD about three times longer than the average student by the time they have settled down and then been distracted a few times. Their families may sometimes struggle all evening to keep them on target. So decide which parts must be done and what is optional.

o Give clear instructions, verbally as well as written.

o Make sure the homework is written down correctly or fastened securely if on a printed sheet.

o Older students may like to record the instructions electronically if they are allowed to use mobile phones or other devices in school. These are much less likely to be lost than homework diaries.

o Make some homework fun and different. Can you set word searches, quizzes, computer exercises and creative tasks? Remember that students with ADHD love the 'fun factor'.

Marking

o Decide which things are important for a particular piece of work and mark accordingly. If it is for creative writing, mark for content and try not to worry too much about handwriting or spelling.

o Try to give positive comments.

o Give constructive suggestions for improvement next time.

o Be aware of effort and progress.

o Avoid red pen.

Outside the classroom

It is helpful to understand what happens to the student before and after your lesson. Sometimes it can explain a lot.

Break and lunch times

These unsupervised times can be difficult for students with ADHD as they often find unstructured social situations with other children tiring and unpredictable. They find it hard to play informally with others, and arguments and fights can occur. The student could be the butt of jokes or may be provoked by others. Staff on duty should be on the lookout for bullying behaviour. A few strategies may help:

o Encourage companionship of a sensible 'buddy' to do a joint activity.

o Encourage them to attend a club, society, sports practice or music or art session at these times.

o Suggest they help with younger pupils' activities.

Games lessons

Students with ADHD may have excess energy to burn off. Regular sport and exercise can be an excellent channel for this and should be encouraged.

Fast action sports such as football can be very popular, especially with adult supervision to ensure that rules are observed. Informal, playground 'kick about sessions' can end in conflict. Some team sports, such as cricket, are less suitable as they require sustained concentration, especially when fielding.

Solo sports such as swimming, running, tennis, judo and taekwondo have been shown to be to be very successful for students with ADHD and if possible, these should be encouraged. Taking a sport to a high level can offer challenges and rewards and encourages a disciplined attitude to training. Competing is stimulating and winning gives an instant reward of success.

Personal, social and health education (PSHE) lessons or tutor time

These can be valuable times to discuss issues with the whole class, for example:

o Embracing individual differences

o Tolerance

o Anger management – some role-play might be helpful

o Friendship, kindness

o Body language, social communication

o Bullying

o Depression.

This may offer an opportunity to tell the class about ADHD, but it would depend on the wishes of the student and how comfortable they are talking about it.

- - - - - **View from the inside** - - - - -

When most people get angry they can choose whether they explode - go into a dark tunnel - or flick the points, change direction and find another way to go. For me the tracks go straight into the tunnel - there are no diversions. It's dark; it's black and bad things happen.

After meltdown I feel really upset because I didn't want anything bad to happen but there was nothing I could do to stop it.

Taken from Daniel's story in The Boy from Hell: Life with a Child with ADHD *with kind permission from the author Alison Thompson*

Exams (see Chapter 10)

Students with ADHD may need special arrangements for exams. This could be extra time, rest breaks or the use of technology. It may be appropriate to have a separate room away from other distractions, which also allows a student to move around in order to help concentration. This will depend on the student's needs and their specialist assessor's advice. The SENCO and exams officer will put this in place. The student should be allowed to practise with these arrangements in school exams.

How is ADHD treated?

ADHD is a medical condition and so the child's GP or paediatrician should be monitoring the student's treatment. Here I will merely briefly mention the current trends in treatment.

Medications (neurostimulants) are often used as this can improve concentration by increasing brain activity in the frontal lobe area. This produces calmer behaviour and greater focus, allowing the student to concentrate and learn.

Cognitive behavioural therapy (CBT) has also been shown to be helpful as it teaches the student how to recognise symptoms and manage their behaviour.

Controlling diet and reducing sugar intake has been shown to help keep children calmer in some cases, but the evidence is not conclusive. Food colourings and additives may also be implicated.

Relaxation techniques can help.

Individual help

An *adult mentor* can provide a lifeline for a student with ADHD. They can meet with them regularly, help them to plan and organise their school life, and solve problems as they arise. Celebrating success and progress is another important role that a mentor can fill. Depression is common with students with ADHD and so it is important that they learn to believe in themselves, to become more happy and confident individuals.

A *learning support teacher* can help the student deal with academic needs as they arise. Ideally they should have regular sessions.

Open communication between the student, their mentor, the subject teachers and the learning support teacher provides the most effective overall support that the student needs.

Feedback to parents

Usually this is via a named member of staff, often either the mentor or year head, and class teachers can communicate via this person. Regular feedback to parents is important, so remember to pass on your comments. Make sure that you pass on good news as well as bad. It is great for parents to hear about achievements and accolades as well as areas of concern. It makes it easier for them and reinforces the idea that the teachers and parents are working together.

– – –Key points – – – – – – – – – – – – – – – –

* ADHD is a lifelong medical condition affecting behaviour. It is characterised by inattention, hyperactivity and impulsiveness.

* ADHD affects around 5 per cent of the population.

* Hyperactive ADHD is more commonly diagnosed in boys, although girls are more likely to have the inattentive type, which is harder to identify.

* Teaching style needs to be dynamic and multisensory, with frequent changes of activity to engage students with ADHD since they have a short attention span.

* Students with ADHD will need help with organisation and planning.

* Work should be set as short, manageable tasks.

* Teachers should have a consistent approach with clear classroom discipline.

* Students with ADHD are most successful when there is a whole-school policy on support and discipline and if there is a designated adult mentor.

* Students with ADHD find school tiring and often difficult, but good teacher support can make a huge difference.

Chapter 7

Autism Spectrum Disorder (ASD) and Asperger Syndrome

133

What is ASD?

People with a diagnosis of ASD find it difficult to interpret the behaviour and conversation of others and they are said to have *communication and social difficulties.*

Recently the American Psychiatric Association (2013) modified the ASD diagnosis, and it is now based on two areas of impairment:

○ Social communication and interaction

○ Restricted, repetitive patterns of behaviour, interests or activities.

The severity of ASD can vary along a continuum from mild to very severe.

What is Asperger Syndrome?

Until recently people on the autism spectrum who had normal intelligence and language development were identified as a separate diagnostic category called *Asperger Syndrome.* Some students will still have this diagnosis but in future they will simply be diagnosed as having mild ASD (level 1). It affects around 1–2 per cent of the population and both sexes, but was identified more commonly in boys.

As the term 'Asperger Syndrome' is used colloquially and understood by parents, clinicians and other professionals, it is likely that both terms will continue to be used for some time. As this chapter will be referring only to students with ASD in mainstream education and in the normal to high intelligence range, I will use both terms throughout this chapter.

Where does the name come from?

Hans Asperger was a Viennese paediatrician who identified a group of more able boys on the autism spectrum. They showed behavioural and communication problems but also a range of abilities; their speech and intelligence were in the normal to high range. His paper of 1944 identified this group as having a separate and milder form of autism but with recognisable difficulties in three areas: *communication, socialisation* and *inflexibility of thought.*

During the 1990s both the World Health Organization and the American Psychiatric Association agreed that people with Asperger Syndrome formed a separate group within the autism spectrum. However, the latest thinking is that the boundary is not sufficiently clear between high-functioning ASD and Asperger Syndrome, so they are now grouped together again.

– –

Strictly speaking ASD is not a Specific Learning Difficulty (SpLD) but a medical condition that is usually diagnosed by a paediatrician. Special provision should, however, be put in place in school and teachers made aware of a student's behavioural differences and learning style preferences. Students may be eligible for special exam arrangements.

Some students with ASD may also have other additional SpLDs such as dyspraxia or ADHD, but many will not.

How can I spot a student with ASD/Asperger Syndrome?

These students may appear rather 'odd' and socially isolated. Look for the student who speaks in a rather pedantic way, often using long and complicated words. They may have a great interest in a particular topic and love to discuss it in detail. They often like to talk to adults and may try to have a conversation with you during a lesson (oblivious of the needs of other students). They may have a very rigid outlook and dislike change. They prefer to work alone and may wish to go into unexpected depth on certain topics, but can appear to struggle with more basic work. They do not fit in with the crowd and often have little desire to do so.

When I first met Sarah, a Year 7 student, she arrived in the biology lab early, came straight up to me and announced, 'I don't like arachnids, I have arachnophobia!'

Author

Common indicators

DOWNSIDES

Speech

- Often monotonal and lacking inflection.
- May have a vast vocabulary.
- Uses long, complex words and pedantic language.
- Little use of peer group jargon, or it is used inappropriately.
- Will talk in great detail about a topic of interest.

Conversation

- o Finds it difficult to have a light-hearted conversation. Would prefer a meaningful discussion to 'small talk'.
- o Does not know when to start or stop speaking. May interrupt, or launch into a monologue.
- o Prefers adult conversation.
- o Very literal interpretation of words and phrases.
- o Does not pick up on information expressed through facial expressions or body language.
- o Finds it difficult to understand jokes or puns.
- o Does not pick up implied or inferred information.
- o Finds people's reactions unpredictable and confusing.
- o Cannot easily understand irony, sarcasm and metaphors.
- o Finds idioms confusing unless they are explained.

Social interaction

Students with ASD may find other people confusing and unpredictable as they find it hard to understand the social norms and unwritten behaviour patterns.

> Most people in social situations understand what the rules are automatically, almost by osmosis. If you have Asperger you don't get the rules unless you are told what they are.
>
> *Student*

Here are some of the reasons:

- o Difficulty reading social cues and understanding how others think.

- Unlikely to pick up on unspoken signals indicating whether they are intruding or welcome.
- May invade personal space or keep too distant.
- There can either be a lack of eye contact, which is disconcerting and results in missing facial cues, or too much eye contact, which appears intimidating.
- Will not know how to respond to emotion in others and may react inappropriately.
- Difficulty understanding the expected norms of behaviour when interacting with diverse groups of people such as family, peers or adults in authority. Might be too formal with peers and over-familiar with staff.
- May be the butt of jokes or bullied as they are seen to be different and socially awkward.
- May have very different interests from peer group.
- Does not see the point in just following the crowd.
- Inflexible attitude and opinions. Liable to argue.
- Often very honest and will appear to 'tell tales' which can land others in trouble.
- Will give an honest opinion, which is not always welcome. Has not learned the art of tact to avoid hurting people's feelings.
- Can unintentionally cause offence.

– – – – – – – Theory of mind – – – – – – –

Most children by the age of around five can read social cues so they can understand the thoughts, feelings and intentions of other people and they can predict what people will do next. The psychological term for this is *theory of mind*. This skill allows them to develop empathy with others and to see things from a different point of view. People with ASD have great difficulty reading social cues and understanding how others think, and so they can find social situations confusing and tiring.

- -

Order and routine

A student with ASD:

○ Likes routines, timetables and order.

○ Will have personal routines, following the same route to a classroom and likes to sit in the same place. Familiarity and routine provide security and reduce stress.

○ Dislikes change and unpredictability – can be very upset by a sudden alteration.

○ Arranges items in an exact or particular way, such as coloured pens in a wallet, and will be disproportionally upset if this is altered.

○ May find 'busy places' such as corridors or changing rooms stressful.

○ Is unhappy about sharing personal items.

○ May have certain repetitive behaviour patterns.

○ May have unusual and repeated body movement (tics), which can become more pronounced in stressful situations.

Special interest topic

A student with ASD:

○ Has a special interest which is often something in a narrow field.

o Will research the topic keenly and can be exceptionally knowledgeable about it.

o May change special interest topics as they mature.

o Will talk excessively about a special interest to the point of boring other people.

o Likes spending time doing their special interest as it is ordered, relaxing and secure.

- -

You have very specific interests. Things you really enjoy. They are comforting. It is sometimes easier to talk to adults about them than other children who aren't interested like you are.

Student

- -

o May have *collections of items* which are important. These can be unusual objects such as batteries and keys, or more generally accepted collectables such as model trains, fossils or cards. It can provide comfort to go through the collection, putting the familiar objects in order.

Coordination

Not all students with ASD have coordination problems but many do. A student with ASD may have:

o An unusual walking gait.

o Motor coordination difficulties (similar to those seen in dyspraxia).

o Gross motor skill problems – balancing, catching a ball, riding a bicycle.

Handwriting and fine motor skills may cause difficulty.

Sensitivity (see also pages 92-3 and 146-7)

Students with ASD can be either unusually over- or under-sensitive to certain stimuli (light, sound, smell, taste, touch).

Working with others at school

Working with others is not easy for students with ASD. This is due a combination of poor social skills and an inflexible attitude. A student with ASD:

○ Gets set on a particular idea or approach and finds it hard to compromise.

○ Feels strongly that their ideas are correct.

○ Likes to be in charge and can become bossy or appear arrogant.

○ Has difficulty seeing another person's point of view.

○ Finds it hard to predict other people's reactions.

○ Has problems sharing resources.

○ Finds group situations tiring so feels a need for quiet time on their own.

Temper

Frustration, a sense of unfairness, sensory overload, tiredness or the irrationality of others can lead to strong temper outbursts. This can result in injury to others or themselves. Strategies should be put in place, within school, to deal with a situation if it arises.

Depression

Depression can be a problem for intelligent students with ASD. They are aware that they are different but attempts to fit in socially or to make friends are often rebuffed. Friends are valued in the teenage years, and social rejection can lead to increased isolation and unhappiness.

Common strengths

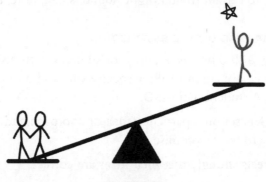

UPSIDES

- Refreshingly honest.
- Will follow rules and may try to make others do the same.
- Likes fairness – often has a strong sense of right and wrong.
- Punctual and reliable.
- Good focus on topics of interest – likes to understand the facts fully.
- Very observant.
- Can have excellent focus on detail.
- Good vocabulary.
- Encyclopaedic knowledge in certain areas.
- Often likes precision planning, timetables, maps.
- Can be very good with electronic or mechanical devices.
- Can excel at logical subjects such as maths or science.
- May be talented in art or music.

- Single-minded.
- Makes decisions based on logic not on social expectation.
- Will not change views 'just to fit in' with the crowd.
- Creative – will often have a very different approach from others.
- Loyal to friends.
- Straightforward, not deceitful or devious.
- Can have a quirky and unusual sense of humour.

Whole-school policy

Ideally in school there should be a designated adult mentor. A student with ASD should meet daily with their mentor who can help them negotiate the challenges of the school day (see 'Individual help' later in this chapter).

There should also be an agreed procedure if the student has a problem in a lesson or break time. They should know who to contact and where to go – preferably a designated quiet room or area where they can go to calm down if there has been a temper incident or just to get some quiet time.

A consistent approach by all teachers to certain norms of behaviour is required, including:

- How to address a teacher or other adults.
- What happens at the beginning and end of lessons.
- Expected standard of behaviour during lessons.
- Expected behaviour in the dining room.
- Where students with ASD can go at breaks and lunch times
- Whole-school policy on bullying.

How can I help in the classroom?

Students with ASD/Asperger can be fun to teach as they bring a different dimension to lessons and a lot of additional insight. They certainly keep you on your toes and will be quick to tell you if you have forgotten something, or made a mistake!

The best approach is to be *very clear and direct* with your speech and instructions. Remember that these students will not pick up implied information or guess what your expectations are so you will have to be explicit.

Your own behaviour

- ° Try to behave in a consistent manner each lesson.

- ° Avoid indirect or rambling speech; make points clearly.

- ° Use short, clear sentences.

- ° Understand that facial expressions and body language are unlikely to be registered.

- ° Do not use sarcasm and remember that humour or irony in your tone will be missed and jokes may not be understood.

- ° Your words could be taken literally so a phrase such as 'return to your desk and do not move' could cause great confusion if they are supposed to be doing a writing exercise. The chances are they will sit there, not doing anything. This is probably not out of defiance or cheek but due to your lack of clarity.

- ° Avoid idioms such as 'pull your socks up'. Students with ASD are likely to interpret them literally.

- ° Give warning of a known change such as having to move classrooms next lesson. Students with ASD like to have prior warning of change.

○ Do not take remarks personally or assume rudeness. Students may not see the point of doing something and tell you so, remind you of an omission or tell you that you are wrong. Remember that they are probably just being honest. Failing to make eye contact can also be misinterpreted as rude or shifty, but it could just be limiting sensory input.

Order and routine in the classroom

○ Have a clear classroom routine. Do the students wait outside the room until you let them in? Do they wait until you tell them to sit down? Where are bags placed? Do you take a register?

○ Have a formal start to your lessons and always begin the same way. This provides structure and tightens discipline, making students with ASD feel more secure.

○ If possible, allow the student to sit in the same place. The end of a row is usually preferred, as this is less hemmed in by others.

○ Explain the aims and outline of the lesson and timings of activities.

○ Keep the room neat and orderly.

○ Ensure that books are be organised on shelves and equipment is in an appropriately labelled drawer or cupboard. It will not be appreciated if the scissors are in the drawer marked glue!

Setting work

○ Give very clear instructions, preferably written. Do not assume anything: include page references, question numbers, exactly what you are expecting them to do, how to lay out the work, if you want it handed in and when it should be finished by.

∘ Tell them when to start if it is a class exercise.

∘ Give time updates – 'There are five more minutes for this'.

∘ On occasion, try to give an opportunity for the student to do something about their special interest. They will enjoy this and it could be a chance for them to shine.

- - - - - **View from the inside** - - - - -

Luke Jackson was only 13 years old when he wrote *Freaks, Geeks and Asperger Syndrome* (2002) in which he gives an amusing but insightful view of school life with ASD. Here are two of his pleas to teachers:

Teachers and support assistants *please* tell the Asperger kids *exactly* what they are expected to get on with.

The key to helping a child on the autism spectrum is to always make sure you tell them very clearly what is going on, I really cannot stress this enough.

- -

Sensitivity

Be aware that some students may be hypersensitive to certain stimuli:

∘ Light: if they have light sensitivity, check their position. Is sunlight streaming in? Does classroom lighting cause a problem? Is the interactive whiteboard too bright? It may be a case of changing the seating, or swapping classrooms with a colleague.

o Noise level: is there a lot of background noise? Electrical equipment or lights buzzing, planes, the central heating system or other students moving or whispering? All these could be very distracting if the student cannot filter out unwanted sounds. Could they wear headphones when working alone? Is there a library or quieter spot to work in?.

o Textures: check if there are any textures that are unpleasant. Sometimes clothes labels or certain materials such as nylon can cause problems.

o Smells: some smells can make people with ASD feel nauseous. Find out if your student is sensitive to any. Care might be needed in cookery, art or science lessons, but also if there has recently been painting done nearby. Perhaps it is also wise to avoid wearing strong perfume or aftershave.

o Heightened sensitivity can mean that students with ASD can be distracted by things that others wouldn't notice such as a crack in the plaster or a ladybird on the window frame. Exciting classroom displays and posters can make it very hard for them to focus on the lesson.

Social integration

Some social skills can be learned by patient reminders and a consistent approach. In your lessons, reinforce expected norms of behaviour and try to encourage sharing of ideas. Encourage all students to listen to each other's ideas.

Temper

o Try to avoid a student temper flare up if possible.

o Be aware of signs of stress and unhappiness.

○ Anger can be the result of an earlier incident at home or school, so they might arrive at your lesson already tense and distressed. It is sometimes worth having a way that students can tell you that they are getting frustrated or angry without flagging it up to the rest of the class.

○ Look for triggers which might cause increased agitation.

○ Try to defuse emotional build up; possibly give them a task to do.

○ Let the student leave the room on some pretext, maybe to go on an errand or to do some 'research' in the computer room or library. Clearly this depends on your subject and the age of the student.

○ Is there a classroom assistant who can help or a designated person for the student to go to?

○ If they are really stressed or aggressive, let them go to the designated quiet room for a bit of 'time out'. Make sure that they know who to report to and remember you will have to tell them when to return to lessons.

○ Keep calm yourself.

Group work

Appreciate that integrating students with ASD into group activities can cause friction. It works better if:

○ you pick the groups

○ each person has a specific role as this reduces argument

○ you supervise carefully.

Look out for unkindness, such as the other group members mocking or bullying the student who may not realise that they are being laughed at. Also check that the student with ASD is not being too dictatorial within the group.

Working alone

Sometimes students with ASD really enjoy the chance to do a solo piece of work. This is OK occasionally, but it should not become the norm. It works best if there are other students who would also like to work alone sometimes.

Homework

Students with ASD find getting through a busy school day extremely tiring and they require some relaxed 'down time' when they get home. They may also have difficulty with the concept of doing more 'school' work at 'home' and resent it. There is an argument for reducing 'homework' where possible or allowing them to fit it in during the school day, perhaps in the lunch hour.

If you set homework:

- Give out homework instructions early in the lesson.
- Explain the work required very clearly.
- Give a written copy of the homework as well as verbal instructions.
- Tell them how long to spend on the homework.
- Explain when should it be handed in and where should it be put.

Project work and essays (see Chapter 9)

Some project work will really play to the strengths of students with Asperger/ASD. They often enjoy research and the difficulty could be stopping them from going into too much detail and coming up with something resembling a thesis.

Certain subjects are easier for students with ASD, for example mathematics, science or history, where the information is logical and ordered. They can find English literature very challenging, as they struggle to see things from other people's perspective so they find it very difficult to answer questions such as 'What was the author thinking about?' or 'What motivated [one of the characters]?'

If English is your subject you will probably need to give very precise guidelines and work with the student to help them interpret questions and learn to answer them in sufficient depth. Ask a series of short closed questions first, to set the background for an essay. An essay plan will be useful (see Figure 9.1 in Chapter 9).

Outside the classroom

It is worth understanding some of the difficulties in school for students with ASD. This may not be directly relevant to your subject but can influence the students' mood and behaviour.

Games lessons

Students with ASD may find class games lessons really hard for the following reasons:

- Poor coordination, so they find team ball sports genuinely difficult.
- Unlikely to be picked by others for a team, which is upsetting.
- May not see the point in team games.
- Dislike of changing rooms and crowds.
- Too much sensory input – shouting, whistles, movement, physical contact, mud.
- The games clothing, mouth guards, shin pads, helmets or goggles may irritate.
- Smells such as chlorine, changing rooms, feet or deodorant may be difficult to cope with.

Sport is undoubtedly good for health, improving coordination and generating a feeling of well-being, so it should be encouraged, but some modifications will make it easier for students with ASD:

o Offset changing room issues by getting the student to arrive a little early to change (see advice on dyspraxia in Chapter 5).

o Consider alternative sports – people with ASD can excel in some more individual sports, for example running, swimming, climbing, dance, cycling, fencing, martial arts, kayaking, sailing, and orienteering.

o Consider giving them another role within the sports department, such as being a linesman, scorer, team photographer or a roving reporter for the school journal.

Dining room

This can be very busy and crowded and extremely stressful. Perhaps the mentor can try to think of strategies to help if this is a problem.

Personal, social and health education (PSHE) lessons or tutor time

These can be useful to discuss issues such as the following with the whole class:

o Embracing individual differences

o Friendships

o Tolerance

o Bullying

o Social communication

o Body language

o Team work.

Students with ASD will undoubtedly benefit from attending these sessions, but they may need to be explained further and reinforced on an individual basis later.

Hobbies and clubs

It is much easier for students with ASD to relate to others if they share common interests: attending clubs and societies can be an excellent way to develop friendships. All the students gain from cooperating in a project that is of mutual interest and benefit.

Clubs such as chess, computer, natural history, space, history and politics can be popular. Joining the technical support crew for drama productions can also be beneficial.

> The highlight of the week for one Year 7 boy was to be allowed to go to the senior chess club. The older students were tolerant and genuinely impressed with his ability.
>
> *Author*

Individual help

An *adult mentor* is invaluable to guide and support a student with ASD. The mentor can help to interpret school expectations and act as a 'go-between' to communicate with subject teachers and solve difficulties as they arise. Misunderstandings are common, and ideally there should be a free flow of information.

The mentor can also help to keep up the student's self-esteem by praising achievement and celebrating success. They should watch out for signs of depression, self-harm, behavioural changes or any indications that the student is being bullied. Taking a genuine interest in the student will make a big difference to their well-being.

A *learning support teacher* will also be able to help in the following practical ways:

- Improving reading body language.
- Teaching implied and inferred meanings.
- Learning to understand expressions, metaphors and meanings.
- Interpreting the meaning of questions.
- Interpreting poetry.
- Helping with the content of essay writing.
- Helping with exam preparation and revision.

Learning support teachers can reinforce work covered in the lessons and lay foundations for new topics. This is most effective when subject teachers liaise with the learning support teacher.

Exams (see Chapter 10)

Special provision may be required. The student may be able to use ICT or take the exam in a quiet room away from the distraction of others. In some cases they are allowed to have extra time or an interpreter to help them to decipher the meaning of the questions. The provision will vary and it will be the role of the school SENCO (special educational needs coordinator) to put this into place with the exams officer.

- - - Key points - - - - - - - - - - - - - -

- ★ People with ASD have difficulties with communication and social interaction. There is a range impairment from severe to mild.

- ★ Asperger Syndrome used to be a separate diagnosis used for people with ASD with normal to high intelligence. This is the equivalent to the new diagnosis of ASD level 1.

★ Students with ASD find other people's reactions confusing and social interaction tiring.

★ They like routine and order and find change unsettling.

★ They will interpret speech literally and not understand implied meaning.

★ They may be very knowledgeable about certain topics.

★ They are honest and loyal but can be rejected and bullied by others.

★ Given the right support they can do well at school.

Chapter 8

Obsessive Compulsive Disorder (OCD)

* What is OCD?
* How can I spot a student with OCD?
* Common indicators
* Common obsessions and compulsions
* Common strengths
* Whole-school policy
* How can I help in the classroom?
* Outside the classroom
* How is OCD treated?
* Individual help
* Key points

What is OCD?

OCD is an *anxiety disorder* that affects boys and girls of school age. One to two per cent of children are diagnosed with OCD. It is a psychological condition which is thought to be related to changes in brain chemistry. Unlike the other Specific Learning Difficulties (SpLDs) discussed in this book it can be treated and controlled with cognitive behavioural therapy (CBT) and sometimes medication. However, this takes considerable time and effort, and the student will need support and understanding throughout. OCD can severely impact school life, academic achievement and relationships.

OCD ranges in severity from mild, which may go undetected, to very severe, where the student might find it almost impossible to leave the house and may need to be home educated for a while.

It is not fully understood what causes OCD but it can run in families, suggesting that there is a genetic link, but environmental factors such as illness or stressful events in a child's life can contribute to the onset of OCD.

OCD often occurs with other problems such as depression, ADHD and autism spectrum disorders (ASD). It is sometimes these other conditions which are identified first.

It is important that teachers understand OCD and how best to help a student who is suffering from this confusing and debilitating disorder. Frequently OCD is not diagnosed for some time and it is generally not well understood.

Where does the name come from?

Obsessions are recurrent anxiety-driven fears. These unwanted thoughts are involuntary, intrusive and irrational, but they are very genuine and cause great stress. Typically these might include severe fear of disease or visions of loved ones being killed or injured.

Compulsions are ritualistic and repetitive actions which are carried out in order to attempt to stave off the terrible fears becoming a reality. Sometimes these actions can seem bizarre, such as repeating phrases or routine or avoiding cracks on the pavement, but the person feels that it is vital to perform these rituals to avoid their feared disasters from occurring.

Both forms of behaviour are part of the OCD condition.

－ －

The OCD cycle

Carrying out the compulsions takes time and energy and only provides temporary relief from the obsessive thoughts. The sufferer may also try to avoid certain situations which they perceive as potentially dangerous. This can affect punctuality, performance and relationships (see Figure 8.1).

OCD Cycle

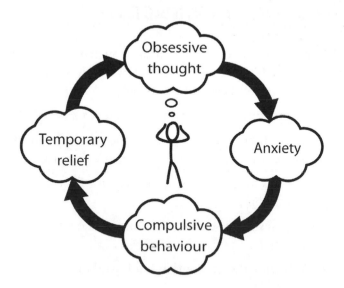

Figure 8.1 The OCD cycle

How can I spot a student with OCD?

Many students are embarrassed by their OCD so they try to hide the symptoms to avoid ridicule. Look out for a student who seems excessively anxious and worried. They may be a perfectionist and be very meticulous about order and tidiness. They may show a dislike of crowds and keep away from others.

Common indicators

DOWNSIDES

A few of the most common indicators which students may show are listed below. Symptoms vary widely so a student may show some of these indicators only.

○ Disproportionately stressed and anxious.

○ Gets 'stuck' on a particular thought or perceived problem and is unable to continue with a task.

○ Anxious to get things right. May ask for reassurance several times.

○ Rewrites work several times and rubs out work done in pencil.

○ Although the student is hard working, homework may be late or incomplete.

○ Becomes distraught at times and might need to leave the room.

- Always arranges pens or equipment in a certain way.
- Likes to sit in the same place.
- Most relaxed with set routines and may panic if these are disrupted.
- Avoids touching others and getting too close.
- May try not to touch door handles, shared keyboards or equipment handled by others.
- Carries out excessive hand washing or uses hand sanitiser.
- Frequent requests to go to the toilet.
- May arrive late for lessons.
- Shows lapses of concentration at times (due to worrying or dealing with obsessions).
- Carries out certain routines or unusual repetitive behaviour patterns.
- Avoids certain 'triggers', perhaps particular numbers, colours or pieces of equipment such as sharp objects which are seen as potentially harmful.
- Habits such as pulling out hair or skin pricking may be noticed.
- All symptoms get worse in times of stress such as the run-up to exams or if there are changes in home life.

Common obsessions and compulsions

These can vary widely in type and severity, but here are a few to look out for. At school these intrusive worries can be very debilitating and affect both work and friendships.

Obsessions

- Contamination: an 'out of control' fear of dirt and germs.

- Need for certainty: excessive worry and checking.
- Harm or danger: to themselves or to others. Frequently there is a fear that loved ones will be hurt or killed.
- Loss: an irrational fear of running out of something perceived as important.
- Need for symmetry and order: almost ritualistic, as things 'have' to be in a certain way to avoid unwanted consequences.
- Need for perfection: a student with OCD might feel that work they produce will never be good enough; written work may be crossed out and redone several times; rubbing out or ripping up work can occur.
- Negative body image: as a result of perfectionism.
- Aggression: worry that they will harm a friend or family member. They may imagine a scene where they commit a violent act and are terrified that they might actually do this.
- Sexual: unwanted fears of making inappropriate sexual actions.
- Superstitions: lucky or unlucky numbers, colours or words can become important.
- Religious: fear being sinful. Religious objects become significant.

Compulsions

- Excessive washing: this can result in a person showering several times a day, hand washing frequently until it causes soreness, and using hand sanitiser.
- Not wanting to touch others or items touched by others such as door knobs or keyboards.

o Avoiding public toilets: wiping down toilets with disinfectant wipes (difficult to do at school).

o Refusing to share food or use communal eating utensils.

o Insisting on clean clothes and bed linen daily.

- -

> After I had washed my hands at school I would have to nudge the tap off with my wrist, so that I did not have to touch the tap or anything else that other people may have touched with dirty hands.
>
> *From* Touch and Go Joe: An Adolescent's Experience of OCD *by Joe Wells*

- -

o Checking items several times: for example, is all the games kit in their bag?

o Repeating: re-reading instructions several times, rewriting work, repeating routine activities.

o Seeking reassurance: the need for certainty and perfection can lead to students repeating questions several times in order to seek clarification and calm worries. This can be frustrating for teachers and peers as lessons are interrupted.

o Avoidance: students with OCD may be so worried about the possibility that they may carry out aggressive or sexually inappropriate acts that they will avoid situations where they feel that there is any risk that these terrible acts might occur. This limits social interactions with friends and family.

o Arranging things: some ordering behaviour is normal and commendable, but a student with OCD may need to have books or pens ordered in a certain way before they can begin to work.

○ Numbers and symmetry: some students will have a need for symmetry and balance. They will therefore dislike uneven numbers of objects or written odd numbers. This can cause severe problems with schoolwork.

○ Hoarding against the fear of loss.

○ Rituals: many OCD compulsions will involve rituals such as counting and touching items in a specific order or repeating a set phrase a certain number of times in a set place. Counting words on a page or bricks in a wall or having to go three steps up for every two down before being able to continue is time consuming and tiring.

○ A trigger is something that initiates anxiety and an obsessional thought. This leads to the perceived 'need' to carry out a behaviour routine or compulsion. It can be something as simple as sharing a pencil or touching a door knob that triggers a contamination fear. If it is not possible to carry out the compulsion to counteract the fear it will cause great stress and even panic.

Typical comments from students with OCD

My obsessions and compulsions really affect school; when the scary thoughts pop up in my head, it's really hard to concentrate and I get so scared, all I can think about is that I need to do my rituals as soon as possible otherwise something bad is going to happen.

I can't keep up with work and don't get to chill out with my friends as much because of my thoughts and rituals.

Thanks to Dr Amita Jassi, principal clinical psychologist, National Specialist OCD Clinic, London

Common strengths

UPSIDES

As OCD affects students of all types and academic abilities it is difficult to generalise where their strengths lie. Students may, however, show some of the following qualities:

○ Sensitive

○ Thoughtful and caring about others

○ Kind to younger children

○ Orderly and well organised

○ Perfectionist: will aim high and work hard. Can produce excellent work.

○ Accurate and careful

○ Have a good eye for detail

○ Talented in art, music or sport.

Whole-school policy

Psychological problems are often not as openly discussed as physical problems, and the family or student themselves may be reluctant to share the information with the school. There are confidentiality issues and the wishes of the individual and family come first.

However, it is much easier for the school to be supportive if there is an open dialogue with the student, their parents and the doctor. If the condition has been formally diagnosed and a student and family are happy that the school is involved, it is much more effective to work together as a partnership.

It is important not to embarrass the student in front of peers, but a supportive framework should be put in place to help them feel secure and safe. Ideally in school, there should be:

- A designated safe person (mentor) who meets the student regularly.

- A way for the student to contact their mentor if a problem arises during the day.

- A designated quiet place for the student to go to if they need to during the day.

- A clear procedure in place to inform the school office or mentor if there has been a problem.

- Close cooperation between the school and with the student's parents and doctor so the school can be alerted to any changes in treatment.

- Confidentiality – respecting the wishes of the student and family.

- Staff awareness of the possibility of bullying and zero tolerance of it.

Work matters

- Does the student have any other learning difficulties?

- Do they qualify for extra time or rest breaks in tests and exams?

- Can they use a word processor for assignments and exams rather than having to hand write?

- ○ Are there any special arrangements regarding homework?
- ○ Do they have individual learning support lessons?

Medical matters

- ○ Are they taking medication and how might this affect them?
- ○ Are they undergoing CBT sessions? Should workload be lower at this time? The student's doctor or therapist would advise on this.
- ○ Are there any other medical issues that the school is aware of?

If the student has to leave a lesson due to stress or a panic attack:

- ○ Who should be contacted?
- ○ Is there a specified place that the student could go to if they have to leave a lesson?
- ○ Is there a colleague in a nearby room who could help you either with the student or the rest of the class if the student becomes very upset or their anxiety causes an outburst?

Uniformity across all staff about expected norms of behaviour is important and will make it much easier for both the student and the staff to work together.

How can I help in the classroom?

Your attitude and approach are important. Make it clear that you believe in the student and their ability, and you are not judging them by their OCD.

- Be kind and approachable and remember that they are not being deliberately difficult or lazy.

- Keep calm and be consistent in your manner.

- Understand that OCD obsessions can disrupt concentration and cause internal distractions. This will slow performance and the student may appear to be inattentive and anxious at times.

- Be prepared to listen to the student and take their worries seriously. Do not belittle their anxiety or say phrases like 'try to pull yourself together,' but find out if there are any practical ways to help alleviate anxiety in your lessons.

- Let them know that they can come and talk to you individually at an agreed time.

- Remember that most students with OCD really want to do well.

- Keep relaxed and cheerful – a smile goes a long way.

Planning lessons

- Have a set routine for the start of lessons as this is reassuring and provides structure and security.

- Make it clear that the classroom is a safe place where you expect everyone to make mistakes as this is part of learning; this might help other students as well.

- Outline the aim of the lesson, the structure it will follow and the way that the time will be divided during the lesson.

- Give a warning a few minutes before changing activities.

- Provide a checklist so the student can tick off tasks as they are completed. This gives a secure framework.

○ Use a multisensory approach to keep the lesson dynamic and engaging.

○ Make the material as relevant as possible to real-life issues.

○ Be sensitive to the student's fears and worries. Try to avoid any triggers.

○ If any group work is to be done, make sure that you choose the groups or pairs carefully.

Seating

○ A seating arrangement with rows can be less stressful than sitting around tables facing other students. Compulsive behaviours are also less likely to be noticed and commented on by others.

○ Let the student sit at the end of a row rather than the middle as they will feel less trapped.

○ If they have separate tables or desks, try to allow space around their desk if possible.

○ Allow them to use the same desk each lesson.

○ Leave a clear exit route to the door if they need to leave.

○ Let them sit in a position where you can have eye contact. This allows you to see how they are getting on without drawing undue attention to them. You can see if they become distracted or restless. They will also be able to signal to you discretely if anxiety is growing or they need to leave the room.

Embarrassment with peers

Students are often embarrassed and do not want to lose face in front of others, so it is very important that you do not draw undue attention to them or to any unusual behaviour patterns they may have.

- o Do not tease the student or mock their behaviour, even in a light-hearted way.

- o Do not tolerate any teasing or negative remarks from their peers.

- o If they arrive late for a lesson, let them come in quietly and without criticism. It could be that they have had to carry out a time-consuming compulsion on the way.

- o Talk to the student and develop a signal that they can use if they feel the need to leave the room due to a build-up of panic.

- o Know what the procedure should be if they do leave the room. Do they go to the 'safe person' or a quiet place such as the library? It could be that spending just a few moments outside the room is enough to regain control and they can come back and continue.

- o Let them leave your lesson a few moments early at the end to reduce stress caused by crowded corridors or changing rooms.

Triggers

If you know the triggers that cause them anxiety and panic attacks you can try to avoid potentially volatile situations. For example, if they have a fear of contamination, do not expect them to share equipment or wear communal lab coats or sports bibs.

Positive feedback, celebrating success

- o Praise is important for all students but especially those with OCD who suffer badly from self-doubt.

◦ Acknowledge effort and progress.

◦ When marking written work give positive feedback if possible. Turn negative points into constructive ideas for next time.

◦ If the student has a particular talent, for example poetry, try to find occasional opportunities to let them use this skill and shine, as this is good for their morale. If their work can be displayed or read out, this would also be encouraging.

◦ Facing up to fears or not carrying out compulsions is also a major success. If you are aware that they are doing this, a quiet word of praise would be appreciated. Do not draw attention to them in front of the rest of the class, though, as the student may be very embarrassed.

Homework

Be aware that students with OCD may take much longer completing a piece of work than other students. This may be due to compulsive behaviour, such as having to have everything 'just right' in order to start. Alternatively, they might be dissatisfied with the work so start several times. Other unusual compulsions such as counting every word on a page before turning over can also severely hamper progress.

◦ Set small amounts of homework so that it is manageable.

◦ Give out written instructions for homework or classwork.

◦ Do not reprimand the student in class for late or incomplete homework.

◦ Allow more time for longer assignments to be completed and ask to see small sections over an agreed timeframe.

- Allow the use of electronic software where appropriate.

- Try to be flexible, especially if the student is undergoing CBT sessions. These can be exhausting and it may be better to abolish or greatly reduce homework at this time.

Marking

- Give positive feedback where possible.

- Be constructive with your comments.

- Do not put too much emphasis on grades.

- Reward effort and progress.

- Celebrate good work.

- Avoid red pen.

Dealing with compulsions in lessons

- If they are relatively minor routines you can ignore them rather than draw attention to the student, as long as they are not disruptive.

- Look out for any unusual and repetitive behaviour patterns. These could be new compulsions. It would be worth passing the information on to the SENCO or mentor.

- Be aware of signs of stress building: it is upsetting for everyone if an outburst occurs and it results in the student losing face with their peers. Try to diffuse a situation if you are aware that anxiety is building up – send them on an errand or just allow them to go out for a few minutes.

Tests and exams

OCD symptoms tend to get worse in times of stress, and so students with OCD may find exam times especially difficult. For public exams the SENCO and exams officer will take advice from the student's doctor. It could be that some special arrangements will be allowed:

o Extra time to alleviate anxiety.

o Rest breaks if the tension build-up becomes too great.

o A separate, quiet place to take exams. This could reduce stress and prevent embarrassment caused if others witness any repetitive compulsive behaviours which may be performed.

For internal tests and exams the advice of the doctor and SENCO should be followed. It may be that the student should take modified papers away from the other students.

Outside the classroom

School life can be a great strain for students with OCD and they may feel worried and anxious at several points in the day. Every student with OCD is different and their triggers and anxieties will vary. The ways of helping them will also differ and a flexible approach is essential. Below are just a few suggestions.

Breaks and lunch times

These busy unstructured times can be particularly difficult, especially if the student worries about proximity to others or has anxieties about unpredictable occasions. They might be happier going to a library or having a specific role in a supervised club.

Minor timetable adjustments such as going into lunch a little early, with a friend, can be helpful to avoid crowds. Is a packed lunch an alternative to school lunch?

Games lessons

Contact sports can be very difficult for some students. Encouraging them to help as an official, such as a scorer, linesman or photographer, may be a way to involve them without them having to take part in the games.

Busy changing rooms and dirty PE kit can cause anxiety. Allowing the student to change a few minutes early or in a different place could help.

Science, design technology and cookery

Using sharp instruments, powerful chemicals or lighting ovens or Bunsen burners can be extremely worrying. If this is the case a sympathetic approach by the teacher is important. It might be a time when a buddy system works well – if the student has a supportive partner, the jobs can be divided sensitively between them.

Personal, social and health education (PSHE) lessons or tutor time

It can be very useful to discuss with the whole class a variety of issues that will apply to many of the students but will be especially useful to those with OCD and other psychological problems:

- Embracing individual differences
- Friendship
- Tolerance
- Bullying
- Anxiety
- Depression

- ○ Relaxation techniques
- ○ Who to talk to in school about worries – the support offered by school
- ○ Who is there to give advice and help outside school – doctors, therapists, psychologists
- ○ Mental health issues.

More typical comments
_ _ _ _ . from students with OCD . _ _ _ _

I always get in trouble for not listening.

Some other kids in my school pick on me because they notice when I am doing my rituals... I try to control it, hide it or try not to think about it - but it's really hard.

Some days I don't go to school at all and pretend I am sick or I get in so late because of my OCD delays me in the morning.

Thanks to Dr. Amita Jassi

- -

How is OCD treated?

The most effective long-term treatment for OCD has been shown to be cognitive behavioural therapy (CBT). This is a way of retraining the brain to think differently about obsessions and to resist doing the compulsions. It is a lengthy and tiring process but can be successful. A complete cure is unlikely, but people can learn to manage their OCD symptoms and live relatively normal lives.

Sometimes medication is also given. This is usually to increase the activity of the brain chemicals (neurotransmitters). This can reduce anxiety and allow the student to study better and feel more able to tackle CBT. Learning relaxation techniques or yoga can also be useful for some people.

Individual help

Each student with OCD will need careful support and monitoring to enable them to feel valued and to reach their full potential at school.

An *adult mentor* can be vital to a student's welfare and happiness, providing stable support and giving encouragement and praise. A lack of self-esteem and depression are common problems with OCD, and so it is important to acknowledge success and progress.

The mentor can communicate with the student's parents and, provided that they are willing, can update relevant teaching staff about the treatment and severity of the OCD symptoms as these can fluctuate.

A *learning support teacher* can help a student to devise coping strategies to keep up with work and get through the school day. The student can then feel valued and supported in their battle with OCD.

Sensitive and supportive teachers can make a big difference in the life of a student who is battling with OCD.

– – – Key points – – – – – – – – – – – – – – –

* OCD is an anxiety-based condition in which a person experiences recurrent upsetting thoughts and behaviours.

* Obsessions are irrational fears that occur spontaneously and are unpleasant or frightening for the student.

* Compulsions are rituals that the individual feels they have to perform in order to stop the fear from happening.

* OCD affects 1–2 per cent of the school-age population and occurs equally in girls and boys. The severity can vary.

* Students with severe OCD will find school life, work and friendships very difficult to manage.

* Many OCD sufferers will try to keep it secret.

* If OCD is diagnosed the school needs to work in tandem with the student's parents and doctors to maintain the correct level of support.

* OCD can be managed and largely overcome with therapy and medical support.

* Supportive teachers who understand the condition can make a huge difference to the life and success of students struggling with OCD.

Chapter 9

Organisational Skills

* What are organisational skills?

* Why do some students with Specific Learning Difficulties lack organisational skills?

* How can I spot a student lacking organisational skills?

* Common indicators

* Common strengths

* How can I help in the classroom?

* Planning essays and projects

* Individual help

* Key points

What are organisational skills?

The *Cambridge English Business Dictionary* (2015) defines organisational skills as 'the ability to use your time, energy and resources, in an effective way so that you achieve the things you want to achieve'.

There are three aspects to being well organised:

○ *Physical:* reducing clutter, having a tidy workspace, filing notes and books in a logical and accessible way, bringing the right books and equipment to lessons.

○ *Time management:* getting to appointments and lessons on time. Not wasting time but working effectively and then planning in time for enjoying relaxation and sport. Having good organisational skills is about making the best use of time.

○ *Mental:* thinking through priorities and planning how to fit in the required workload. Balancing work with down time for relaxation and exercise. Making 'to-do' lists to keep on track.

Why do some students with Specific Learning Difficulties lack organisational skills?

When students have problems with short-term memory or concentration, it can contribute to a lack of organisation and a trail of lost items, missed appointments, failing to meet deadlines, getting lost and a generally chaotic lifestyle. This in turn increases stress levels and makes students flustered and unable to perform at their best.

Students with dyslexia, dyspraxia, dyscalculia and ADHD often suffer from short-term memory problems and may therefore often seem to be muddled and disorganised. They may also struggle with the executive function skills which include planning and goal setting and so they often fail to think ahead adequately, learn from experience or meet deadlines.

Coupled with this, students with dyslexia or dyscalculia may also misread written instructions or confuse numbers and so make mistakes with times, dates, room numbers and contact details. Students with ADHD may not register instructions properly and they also have difficulty managing time and estimating how long tasks will take. Students with ASD may have problems interpreting the meaning of instructions due to taking them too literally, and this can then lead to misunderstanding.

As a classroom teacher you cannot solve all the organisational problems of every student in your care, but you can help them to cope by giving very clear instructions, dividing tasks into smaller, manageable chunks and being calm and well organised yourself.

How can I spot a student lacking organisational skills?

These are the students who may arrive late and flustered to lessons, fail to hand in homework on time or do the wrong homework. They may forget to bring the correct equipment to lessons and miss meetings that are not part of their regular routine.

They may also stagger around carrying a very heavy book bag as they are worried about not having the right books and equipment so try to carry everything.

Common indicators
Arriving at lessons

- Often arrives late and flustered.
- Forgets to bring equipment, books, notes, homework.
- Loses files, books and equipment.
- Has difficulty keeping files in order; papers are often muddled chronologically and between subjects.
- School bags can be too full.
- May drop books and equipment on the floor while unpacking and searching for things.
- Books may be bent, torn or muddy due to stuffing too much into a bag, dropping them or standing on them by mistake!

Short-term memory difficulties and organisation

- Cannot remember a list of items, set of instructions or a routine.
- Forgets names, places, numbers and times.
- If visual memory is affected, they may forget what they are writing down when they look down from the board so they may have incorrect instructions.
- Forgets what to do for homework.
- Does homework but forgets to hand it in or cannot remember where to put it.

Time keeping

- Has difficulty telling the time using an analogue clock.
- Gets distracted and loses track of time.
- Fails to judge how long a task will take.
- Misreads information, mistaking the time or day of an event or deadline.
- Often arrives late for appointments, or is so worried about being late, may arrive very early.

- -

My record is arriving a week early to invigilate an exam!

Author

- -

Getting to places

- Instructions or directions may be forgotten or muddled.
- Can misread times, timetables and instructions.
- Easily gets lost as cannot remember a route.
- May confuse left and right – poor sense of direction.

- ○ Muddles names of places and people, especially if they begin with the same letter.

- ○ Liable to go to the wrong room at the right time or to the correct room at the wrong time.

John rarely used his locker as he often couldn't find it during the first term at secondary school and was too exhausted to walk back to it when he did vaguely learn where it was.

Mother of a dyspraxic teenager

Organising thoughts

- ○ Problems putting ideas into logical sequences.

- ○ Liable to get sudden thoughts which are relevant but at a tangent to the original idea.

- ○ Forgets ideas rapidly if they are not recorded.

- ○ May be good practically but has trouble putting ideas on paper.

Planning projects

- ○ Overwhelmed by large pieces of work as they seem daunting.

- ○ Does not know where to start.

- ○ Has difficulty allocating time to the different sections of a project so will spend too long on one part and has little time for the rest of it.

- ○ Holistic thinker so may get too many ideas very quickly covering a whole topic and not be able to compartmentalise.

- ○ Procrastinates, puts off starting and then panics as a deadline approaches.

Common strengths

These will vary depending on the reason for the disorganisation and will not apply to everyone. However, I have found the majority of my disorganised students show some of the following traits:

- ○ Often very charming.

- ○ Friendly and outgoing, may be entertaining and amusing.

- ○ Good verbally, may be powerful speakers.

- ○ Passionate about subjects or causes.

- ○ Lateral thinkers.

- ○ Innovative.

- ○ Creative.

- ○ Entrepreneurial.

- ○ Strong at drama, music or art.

- ○ Doggedly determined.

How can I help in the classroom?

Your attitude is the most important thing. Disorganised students can be infuriating, but if you become cross or sarcastic they will only become more flustered and disorganised as they begin to panic. The best tactic is to keep your sense of humour and let them know that you will work with them to find some solutions to their problems.

Be approachable so that they feel that they can come and see you, especially if they get behind with their work. Many students are afraid to talk to teachers as they fear that they will be in trouble, the situation then gets worse and they get to a work crisis point. Some will then either pretend to be ill to avoid particular lessons, or become genuinely ill with worry.

It can be useful to have a set time when you are available in your teaching room for students to come and see you in a more relaxed atmosphere than in a lesson. Disorganised students will often opt to come and do their homework during the day in the classroom. This ensures that the work gets done and then it can be handed in immediately before it gets forgotten or lost.

Work with the student and plan the best tactic for both of you.

Classroom matters

o Have spare copies of textbooks, writing equipment, calculators and paper in your classroom. These can be lent out, saving the student stress and anxiety and avoiding missed lesson time while they go back for something which they might not be able to find anyway.

o Have clearly labelled shelves for handing in work.

o Colour-code your subject folders, textbooks and your shelf to hand books in. Stickers can be used.

o Have the shelves and cupboards in your teaching room clearly labelled with a logical system. This is especially important in a practical subject such as art, science or design technology for getting out equipment and putting it away.

o If a student is using a computer in lessons, make sure that a printer is easily accessible.

o Check that material recorded electronically can be safely stored and retrieved.

o Have a clock (preferably digital) clearly visible and use a timer to indicate how much longer there is for a particular task within the lesson. Electronic timers can be set to count down as a task progresses.

The computer site for teachers, 'eChalk' has a great timer
which can be set to make a different noise at the end. My
classes sometimes voted to choose the final noise. The
winner was invariably the belch!

Homework

- Make sure that your instructions are very clear.

- Give out the homework early in the lesson, not right
  at the end.

- Try to give out written copies of homework as well as
  verbal instructions.

- Fasten any paper instructions into the student's
  homework book or file.

- If they have written it down, check that it is correct.

- Could they put homework or other reminders onto
  a mobile phone? This is much less likely to get lost
  than a homework book.

- Is there a school intranet where you could put the
  homework? Could it be emailed to the student?

- Try to find a 'buddy' who they can contact in the
  evening if they have forgotten the homework.

- Ideally keep to a routine about when homework
  is set, when it is due to be handed in and where it
  should be put.

- If homework can be done electronically it can be
  emailed to you. This is less likely to get lost.

Getting around school

Usually in secondary schools the teachers have set rooms and the students move from lesson to lesson. This can be very confusing for someone with dyslexia if they have a poor sense of direction.

○ Clearly label your teaching room door, especially if it is in a long corridor. Colour helps here, or a picture relevant to your subject.

○ If possible, check at the end of the lesson that the student knows where they are going next. This is especially important when they are new to the school or it is a new academic year and timetable.

○ A buddy system may be useful to help them to get to lessons on time in the right place.

○ Ideally the student should have been given a map of the school site and a colour-coded timetable with subject rooms marked on it.

Planning essays and projects

These can seem very daunting. Holistic learners will see the enormity of the whole task, find it overwhelming and not know where to start. More sequential thinkers can end up focusing on one aspect in too much detail and not get the balance and perspective of the whole project.

It's important to give very clear instructions. The following pointers may be helpful:

○ Give a clear title.

○ Explain how to structure the piece of work (see Figure 9.1):

   i.   *Introduction:* this should briefly outline the key topics to be discussed in the main body of the essay but not give any specific detail.

ii. *Main body:* each paragraph should be one point plus evidence; it should begin with a topic sentence which shows what is to follow. The rest is evidence or detail relating to that topic and follows in the next few sentences.

iii. *Conclusion:* this should round off the work. It should be short and not include new ideas. This should refer back to the title. Generally the advice is to keep this short and summarise key points relating back to the title.

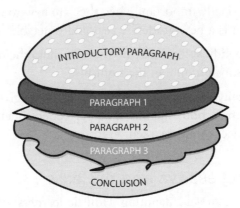

Figure 9.1 An essay burger

o How long do you want the essay to be? Indicate roughly the number of pages or words.

o Stress the importance of writing an essay plan before starting. Emphasise the need to plan before embarking on the work in order to keep to the point and to give the essay a structure.

o An essay-planning table can be a useful way to help the student to structure an essay and decide what to include in each section or paragraph (see Figure 9.3).

o If it is a comparison, both sides of the case must be presented.

○ Emphasise the importance of relating to the title.

○ Divide longer projects into smaller manageable chunks and give dates when different sections are due. Ask for all the sections to be handed in at specific times so that you can check that students are on target.

○ Be clear about when the whole project should be completed.

○ How should it be handed in? Can it be emailed to you? Must it be a paper copy? Where should it be placed?

Most students will wish to use computers for projects and coursework assignments. If students do not have permission to type in exams they will need to continue practising hand writing ordinary essays.

Five steps to essay and project success

1. Brainstorm

2. Plan

3. Start writing
   ○ Introduction
   ○ Main bulk of the essay, several paragraphs
   ○ Conclusion

4. Proofread and edit

5. Reread, print and hand in (this is more applicable to major coursework written using a computer).

An example essay title: 'How to succeed in sport'
STEP 1: BRAINSTORM

Students will vary in the way that they like to plan the content of an essay or project.

Linear thinkers are logical, sequential, step-by-step thinkers who may like to produce lists or bullet points with headings. These can then be arranged into the eventual paragraphs. A linear thinker might produce something like this:

Fitness

- Regular gym sessions
- Strength – weights
- Endurance – cardio-vascular, circuits

Health

- Nutrition
- Training
- Sleep

Psychology

- Relaxation
- Attitude
- Celebrating success
- Goal setting

Skill

- Learning new skills
- Practice
- Training

Discipline

- Training
- Diet
- Commitment

For lateral thinkers, ideas may seem to be disconnected and these thinkers may find it much easier to produce a spider diagram or mind map to get their ideas written down before they are forgotten.

Starting with a word or picture in the middle of the page, ideas can be assembled into different areas in 'bubbles' and detail can be added as the diagram develops (see Figure 9.2). It is possible to get advanced computer programs for mind mapping using colour and symbols to make an impact. Some programs will then change the random arrangement of the mind maps into text with a linear sequence of points.

Sport mind map

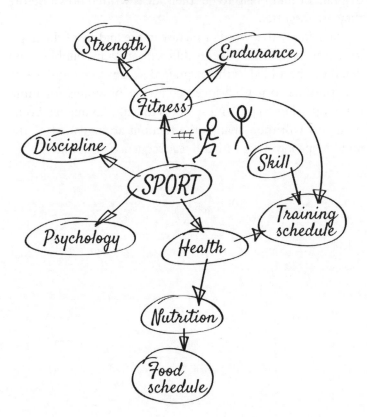

Figure 9.2 A simple Mind Map® for success in sport

There is no right or wrong way and students should be encouraged to get their ideas down in a way that works for them.

STEP 2: PLAN

The ideas then need to be put into a sensible order to answer the question. Remind students of the expected length and the approximate number of paragraphs. A grid similar to that in Figure 9.3 can be helpful here. Ask to see it completed.

This ensures that they do not miss out this stage. This is useful for all students and is a good discipline.

TITLE: Write out the title. Underline or highlight key words. What does the title mean?

INTRODUCTION: What are you going to talk about? What does the title mean?

PARAGRAPH 1:

Main point:

Evidence:

How does this relate to the title?

PARAGRAPH 2:

Main point:

Evidence:

How does this relate to the title?

PARAGRAPH 3:

Main point:

Evidence:

How does this relate to the title?

CONCLUSION: What have you said? Summarise the information. Relate back to the title. Do not include new information.

REFERENCES: If applicable.

Figure 9.3 Planning an essay

STEP 3: START WRITING

- *Introduction:* just getting started is often the hardest part. Many students will procrastinate at this stage and this is why it is helpful to ask to see small sections periodically.

- *Main bulk:* remind students to keep the title in mind and to balance the paragraphs and not concentrate too much on one aspect.

- *Conclusion:* keep this short and summarise key points, relating back to the title.

STEP 4: PROOFREAD AND EDIT

Proofreading is important. Unfortunately, students with dyslexia find it hard to spot their mistakes but they need to practise this art. The spell checker can sometimes come up with strange words that are unintended.

STEP 5: REREAD, PRINT AND HAND IN

A last read through and then hand the work in on time. Some students are perfectionists and will always want to hang on to their work as long as possible.

Use of assistive software

Voice recognition software converts the spoken voice into text. It helps students who struggle with writing or spelling as it allows them to concentrate on the content of what they are saying, rather than the process of writing and spelling.

Advanced spelling correction programs can also be useful. There are now some available for students with dyslexia which are based on phonetics and not on letter patterns. These are less likely to come up with wrong interpretations of the writer's intention.

Individual help

Students who lack organisational skills will benefit from having an *adult mentor* to help keep them on track. Ideally they should meet regularly with the mentor and it is very helpful to invest time putting coping strategies into place to help them with organisation and planning. This support will be needed throughout school as many students come 'unstuck' when they reach the sixth form and they have more freedom.

Here are a few things that work well:

Finding things

- Label lockers and pegs with colour stickers or pictures for easy recognition.

- Make sure all books and personal items are clearly named.

- Periodically help the student to tidy a locker or desk. They will probably be in an unworkable mess.

- Colour-code different subjects' exercise books and textbooks. This can be done with stickers. These can then be easily identified.

- If work is done on file paper, students may need to be shown how to organise their work chronologically. Encourage the use of dividers. Files should be checked and reorganised regularly as they can rapidly become chaotic again.

- Encourage routines for putting things away.

- Make sure the student knows where to go to find lost property.

Getting to places on time

- Provide a simple plan of the school layout with lesson rooms marked.

- Make a copy of their timetable with lessons marked in different colours.

- Check that the student understands how to read the timetable.

- Mark the lesson rooms clearly on the timetable.

- Sometimes it helps to indicate how to get to the rooms, for example History Room 6 (upstairs, first left).

- Make several duplicate copies of the timetable. These can be placed:

  - inside a homework book or diary, glued in
  - inside a locker or desk
  - inside a book bag
  - at home.

  In addition, have one spare with their mentor. Electronic copies of the timetable are excellent if available.

- Teach them to write down and then repeat back any arrangements, times, places, phone numbers, to make sure that they are correct.

- Instructions given electronically are helpful as they can be referred to several times as needed. Pieces of paper often get lost.

Remembering to get to special events or meetings

- If there is a school intranet it is very useful to put details of events, times, dates and places on it.

○ A buddy system can work well if a friend will volunteer to remind students about meetings. It also means that they have someone to go with to avoid getting lost.

○ Can the student be sent an email reminder?

○ Reminders can also be set on mobile phones, if these are allowed in school. These can be set to vibrate as a reminder of an imminent meeting.

Bringing the correct equipment and handing in homework

○ Write on the timetable when PE equipment or musical instruments are needed.

○ Indicate on the timetable when homework is due and where to hand it in.

○ A small notebook can be handy to write reminders in if electronic aids such as phones are not allowed.

○ Encourage the use of sticky coloured paper notes as reminders.

○ Students will sometimes write memos into their mobile phones or record voice reminders.

○ Encourage the use of 'to-do' lists. Having a small whiteboard at home can be useful to write a 'to-do' list on. It is very satisfying wiping off or crossing out when tasks are finished.

A weekly planner may help here in addition to the timetable (see Figure 9.4).

	Mon	Tues	Weds	Thurs	Fri	Sat
Bring to school	Swimming things Trumpet	Games Kit	Games Kit	Trumpet		Paper Round FOOTBALL
Hand in	English French	Maths Geography	ART	Science	History	
Special clubs / lessons	BRASS BAND		football practice	Trumpet lesson	Football Practice	
Homework	Maths Science	History	French	Geography	ENGLISH ART	
After school	Take home wet swim things	Trumpet practice	Trumpet practice	Football club		

Figure 9.4 A weekly planner

Meeting deadlines

Students with executive function difficulties do not find it easy to plan their time and think ahead. They will need to be shown how to set targets, meet deadlines and pace themselves sensibly.

A term planner can be a very useful tool as coursework deadlines, exams, plays, sports fixtures and other important events can be written onto it. Students can then anticipate pressure points when events coincide, for example if the school play is on the week before the history coursework deadline, or a football tournament weekend is the weekend before an art exam.

There are always pressure points in any school term, but it makes it a great deal easier if these can be anticipated and planned for.

Emergency safety nets

○ The mentor can arrange to have a spare pencil case and maths equipment available in a central place in school, possibly the office or staffroom. These can be borrowed in an emergency, for example at exam time. It takes the stress and anxiety away if these things have been forgotten at an important time.

○ Make sure that the student knows where the spare emergency equipment is kept.

○ The student should be able to contact their mentor at set times, to talk through difficulties as they arise. This should be encouraged as early intervention can prevent a crisis point occurring with conflicting deadlines and pressures.

○ Sometimes the mentor will have to be a 'go-between' with other staff members if the student has got out of control with their workload. In order to take the pressure off, it is sometimes sensible to 'wipe the slate clean' and start again with only essential work being tackled. The mentor and SENCO (special educational needs coordinator) could advise here.

- - - Key points - - - - - - - - - - - - - - -

✶ Students with SpLDs often have problems with organisation.

✶ Organisation includes time keeping, bringing the correct equipment to lessons, remembering instructions, and the executive skills of planning and goal setting. Students will have to put special effort into all these areas to succeed, and it will be tiring for them.

* Teachers can help by having spare equipment and a clear system of labelling for books and materials. It also helps if the teaching room is easily recognisable.

* Dividing large projects into small manageable chunks with regular checks helps to guide students through tasks which are seen as daunting.

* Teachers who are approachable, balanced and maintain their sense of humour can help disorganised students enormously. If students feel that they can discuss work and time management problems with a teacher before they hit a work overload crisis, it will provide a 'safety valve' and keep them afloat.

Chapter 10
Exams and Revision

Common pitfalls at exam time are identified:

* Mistiming revision
* What to revise
* How to revise
* Getting exhausted
* Organisation on the exam day
* In the exam
* After the exam
* Key points

Exams are a stressful time for most students, but those with Specific Learning Difficulties (SpLDs) may find them really frightening.

These students may have a history of underperforming, and short-term memory problems will mean that they are unable to do the last-minute cramming that their peers may get away with. This may increase stress and then panic follows. We are all less able to think clearly when the emergency 'fight or flight' response kicks in, and this can increase the chances of errors in reading and interpreting questions. Students can even sometimes go blank and be unable to answer even simple questions on a topic they know well.

As teachers, we can try to reduce exam pressure, where possible, and to help the students to be well prepared, so that there is less last-minute panic.

I will concentrate on the 'pitfalls' awaiting students with SpLDs.

Pitfall 1: Mistiming revision

Some teenagers with SpLDs have problems with planning, learning from experience and thinking ahead (executive function tasks). This means that work is often left to the last minute and accompanying short-term memory problems mean that trying to revise the night before will not result in success.

Students should be encouraged to make a *revision timetable* in the weeks before exams. This should be based on a calendar with the days marked off and divided into blocks for different subjects. Rest and relaxation should also be timetabled in. The days can then be crossed off and progress can be seen and a last-minute panic can be averted.

A very articulate but disorganised student arrived at my door on the morning of her afternoon GCSE Biology exam. After entering and dropping her bag on the floor she said 'Dr Hudson, please could you just go through all the biology that has eluded me over the last two years!' Luckily she did pass and is now happily pursuing a degree in English!

Author

It is also useful to have a large copy of the *exam timetable*, maybe displayed on a wall, so that the order of the exams can be seen at a glance. This allows priority to be given to subjects which occur first, especially if there is some free time in the middle of the exam period. It is also a joy to cross them out once the exams are over!

Pitfall 2: What to revise

Some students (more often girls) will get too bogged down and feel that they have to learn every minute detail and example. Others will have a more superficial, broad knowledge but do not have enough facts and key words in their armoury when it comes to getting marks (more often boys). The art is to aim for somewhere between the two extremes.

I always advise students taking external exams to use the syllabus very closely as a guide. The syllabus outlines exactly what is expected. It will say which definitions must be known and the level of knowledge needed. It is helpful if you provide a list of revision topics to guide internal exam candidates.

Textbooks or revision guides can be helpful as the student's own handwritten notes can be inaccurate or muddled. Learning the key facts and understanding concepts is the aim of revision. Exams are generally based partly on recall and partly on skills which require a clear head on the day.

Pitfall 3: How to revise

The pitfalls here are best illustrated again by the two extremes:

- o The *perfectionist student* might make beautiful 'revision notes' which are virtually the whole subject rewritten. This can take hours to produce and the notes are often attractively illustrated. Sadly, the information is probably no better fixed in the memory as the material has not been condensed or key points emphasised.

○ The *over-confident student* will look over the notes either in their book or on a revision website online. They will not write down anything but feel that they 'know it all'. It comes as a nasty shock on exam day when their lack of detailed knowledge lets them down.

The ideal is to focus on the main points and get them firmly into the long-term memory. Students with short-term memory problems cannot expect much help from a quick read through. The best way to reinforce the facts is to use the student's preferred learning style. A range of ideas are listed in Table 10.1 but each student will need to find what works best for them.

For most people a combination of methods works best. It relieves boredom and keeps the brain actively engaged.

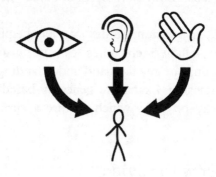

Table 10.1 Learning styles and revision methods

Learning style	Revision methods
Visual	*Left-brained:* Write out bullet point notes; highlight key words; use mnemonics; make posters of phrases, key words or formulae. *Right-brained:* Mind maps; cartoons; drawings; flow charts; timelines; use coloured pen or coloured card; make posters illustrating facts or associated ideas; use computer programs.
Auditory	Listen to tapes of set books; read information aloud; self-record and play back; revise with a friend asking and answering questions; convert facts into song, raps, rhythms, poems.
Kinaesthetic	Use practical examples; let everyday items represent the topic material in order to understand concepts, e.g. a battle scene could be played out with different coloured paperclips; make 3D diagrams; walk about and recite; lie on the floor; stand on one leg to say French verbs; handle equipment; use interactive computer programs.

Revision should be carried out in short blocks of time with breaks for exercise, a snack or a reward. Students' concentration spans vary a great deal but it is better to do several short sessions of 15 minutes than to sit for two hours staring out of the window and thinking of other things. I would suggest that mobile phones are switched off or, preferably, left elsewhere during revision sessions. They are a huge distraction.

It helps to have a few high spots in the programme for each day: 'If I finish my Roman history I can watch my favourite TV programme.'

Going through past papers with mark schemes is also very useful as it teaches students what is considered important and indicates the depth of knowledge required. The mark allocation normally reflects the number of points needed.

Pitfall 4: Getting exhausted

Over-working can be almost as bad as under-working. Students can get tired and stressed and feel overwhelmed by the amount of work. This would especially affect perfectionist students who will be trying to learn everything. Stress can lead to sleep problems, which in turn affect performance and the ability to think clearly and rationally.

Pacing revision and factoring in breaks is important, as is deciding what is essential to learn and which things can be left out.

Last-minute cramming is a bad idea and it is far better to ease off the night before an exam. Students should be encouraged to relax and have an early night.

Pitfall 5: Organisation on the exam day

I have known students who have missed exams altogether owing to misreading the exam timetable. Make sure that they check the date in advance and know whether it is a morning or an afternoon session.

Arriving late can also happen with disorganised students and then they start the exam in a panic. Advise them to allow plenty of time in case there are traffic problems or unforeseen difficulties. Make sure that they know where the exam is being held. This is especially important if they have special arrangements and are not in the main exam room but in another location. They may need to rehearse the route to their exam room.

Remind them to bring the correct equipment. It is always useful to have a spare pencil case, calculator, coloured overlay and whatever else might be needed, in the exam room or school office. It can be lent to a student who forgets something. After all, the exam is based on subject knowledge and not on organisational skills ability.

Pitfall 6: In the exam

Here are some instructions to students taking exams that are often helpful:

- o At the beginning, students should try to relax, wriggle their shoulders and toes, and practise deep breathing.

- o They should read the instructions carefully and underline or highlight key words, answering the right number of questions from the correct sections.

- -

Does the question read: 'Answer 1 question from part A and 3 from part B', 'Answer 2 questions from A and 2 from B' or is it 'Answer all the questions'? Students often fail to follow this sort of instruction correctly and they throw away marks.

- -

○ It is very easy to misread questions, either altering words or missing out key words altogether, especially with a combination of nervousness and dyslexia. Advise students to use a highlighter or to underline key words and to read the question twice. Multiple-choice questions can be especially difficult and almost seem to be designed to try to trip the student up.

I once wrote an excellent answer defining *convection*, complete with diagrams of air flow in colour (I liked science). Sadly, I scored 0 marks. Actually the question was 'What is *convention?*'

Author

○ Exam words: special notice should be taken of leader words in questions and care should be taken to ensure that an answer reflects these. For example, compare, contrast, describe, evaluate, explain, illustrate, state, summarise. It is an idea to go through these terms with students in advance and explain what each one requires.

○ Always plan long answers and essays: jotting down ideas and making rough plans are invaluable strategies, especially for students with short-term memory problems or 'grasshopper minds'. It is then worth rereading the question before starting to write to make sure that the answer is relevant.

○ Timing in the exam: mistiming is a common fault, especially in essay subjects. Some students are slow to write or to process information. Others lose concentration and time passes while they are thinking of other things. Some may give too much detail in one question and then have to rush the others.

Perfectionist students will be loath to move on until an answer is excellent. They may even cross the whole thing out and start again.

- Reading the time: it is best for students to have their own watch or clock, preferably digital, so it won't matter if they can't see the exam clock clearly.

- Check work at the end: students should look out for number reversals in maths answers and check that units are correct.

- Extra time: if this is has been allowed the students must be taught how to use it properly, especially for thinking and planning. They should also have practised with extra time in school tests and exams.

Pitfall 7: After the exam

Avoid conducting a 'post mortem' of the paper with other students. It is too late to do anything about any mistakes and it can cause anguish and undermine self-confidence. It is important to keep morale up and stay cheerful, especially if another exam is imminent.

Avoid dwelling on any mistakes. It is better to move on to the next thing. Most students who lack self-confidence ignore the large number of things that they may have done correctly and worry about any errors.

Encourage the students to relax for a while, to eat and get some fresh air and exercise. This will 'recharge the batteries' and allow clear thinking before the next exam or revision session.

Special arrangements in public exams

Many students with SpLDs will qualify for special arrangements in public exams. They must be officially diagnosed either by a specialist assessor, usually a specialist teacher who holds an Assessment Practising Certificate, or an appropriately qualified educational psychologist. A paediatrician or child psychiatrist may diagnose some conditions such as autism spectrum disorder (ASD).

The rules and special arrangements are complex and change periodically so the school SENCO (special educational needs coordinator) will work with the exams officer to ensure that the provision that has been recommended is carried out. In the UK regulations are printed by the Joint Council for Qualifications (JCQ).

The list of possible special arrangements is long but here are some of the most common ones found in mainstream schools:

○ Extra time (usually 25 per cent, but it can be longer in special circumstances) – this can be for slow writing or processing speed.

○ Supervised rest breaks.

○ Separate invigilation away from the other students.

○ Coloured overlays.

○ Coloured or enlarged papers.

○ A word processor with the spelling and grammar checker disabled.

○ A scribe (amanuensis) – a responsible adult who will write down or word process the candidate's dictated answers, often used when a candidate has coordination difficulties and cannot use a word processor.

○ A reader – a responsible adult who reads the question paper out to the candidate. They are not permitted to explain or interpret any of the paper. Computer software can also be used for this.

○ A candidate who is in a separate room may be allowed to read out loud or walk around the room.

○ A practical assistant – a responsible adult who can give physical support for students with severe coordination difficulties.

○ A prompter – a responsible adult who periodically reminds the candidate of how much exam time is left. This helps students who find it hard to remain focused, those with little sense of time and perfectionists who are inclined to keep improving a question rather than moving on to the next one.

In all the cases listed the student must show a history of using these techniques in their normal lessons and in school exams. This gives them a chance to practise the skills and will provide both a history of need and a history of provision which is required by the JCQ. Classroom teachers should be aware of the provision that is recommended for a student to ensure that the advice is followed as normal classroom practice.

- - - **Key points** - - - - - - - - - - - - - - -

⋆ Exams are especially stressful times for students with SpLDs.

⋆ Planning a revision schedule is important.

⋆ Students must learn revision techniques using their preferred learning style and pace themselves sensibly.

⋆ Exam advice for students:

• students should be advised to check when and where the exams take place

• bringing the correct equipment is important, but it is useful to have spares for emergencies in school

- during exams students must concentrate on reading instructions and questions carefully and take notice of the leader words in questions

- timing and planning are important, especially if a student has extra time

- after exams it is important from students to relax and not to over-analyse any perceived errors.

* Special arrangements can be put in place in public exams.

Chapter 11

A Final Word

Thankfully, many young people who have Specific Learning Difficulties (SpLDs) are now diagnosed early and receive the additional help that they need to negotiate their way successfully through their schooldays. Some are still not spotted, though, and it is often an astute teacher who identifies them. Watch out for discrepancies in a student's performance and, if you are concerned, ask the SENCO (special educational needs coordinator) to investigate further. Girls are especially likely to be missed as they often try to try to blend in with the crowd and pass unnoticed.

There are many stories of people with SpLDs of one sort or another who have gone on to lead happy and successful lives. Some have become inspirational leaders in their fields or forged new ground. If you consider the current entrepreneurs, computer programmers, web designers, actors, film directors, authors, sporting legends, chefs or fashion designers, many of them will be people who have an unusual way of thinking and for whom learning at school was a struggle.

The advantage of thinking differently enables people to see new opportunities and unusual paths to follow. Ultimately it is their thinking differences that help to shape their lives and make them who they are. Their success may well be not 'in spite of' their SpLDs but 'because of' them.

If you, as a teacher, can help these young people to be proud of their strengths and learn how to laugh when things go a little wrong, you will have contributed hugely to launching the adults that they will become. Their SpLDs will never go away but they can learn coping strategies, enabling them to channel their many skills and talents and to maximise their potential.

As teachers, we should encourage these young people who think a little differently, and enjoy their company. I can guarantee that they will be annoying, challenging and frustrating at times, but they may well be the students you will remember most fondly.

Glossary

Amanuensis: A person who writes from dictation. Can be used by students with severe writing difficulties, both in class and in exams.

Asperger Syndrome: People on the ASD spectrum with normal to high intelligence and vocabulary. This is no longer recognised as a separate diagnosis to ASD as the boundaries are not always clear.

Attention deficit hyperactivity disorder (ADHD): A disorder which causes a short attention span, impulsiveness and sometimes increased physical activity (hyperactivity). It is a result of reduced activity in the frontal lobe area of the brain.

Auditory learning: Learning by taking in information that has been heard through speech, song, music and sound recordings from the natural world.

Auditory memory: The ability to remember information that has been heard.

Auditory processing speed: The time to take in information that has been heard, to think about it and be able to respond.

Autism spectrum disorder (ASD): People with a diagnosis of ASD have communication and social difficulties and restricted, repetitive patterns of behaviour and interests.

Cognitive behavioural therapy (CBT): Treatment that aims to solve problems by talking about them with a therapist and gradually changing how people think and behave. It can be useful to treat anxiety and depression, OCD and ADHD.

Compulsion: Ritual behaviour which a person with OCD feels that they have to carry out in order to prevent bad things from happening to themselves or to others.

Computer reader in an exam: Computer software which accurately reads out text, but does not decode or interpret the paper.

Developmental coordination disorder (DCD, also called dyspraxia): A specific learning difficulty involving muscles and fine or gross motor coordination. Symptoms include difficulty with movement as well as problems with organisation, short-term memory and planning.

Dyscalculia: A specific learning difficulty that affects mathematical skills especially arithmetic and counting.

Dysgraphia: A specific learning difficulty that affects handwriting and converting thoughts to written words.

Dyslexia: A specific learning difficulty that affects reading and interpretation of the written word together with spelling and converting ideas into writing.

Dyspraxia: see developmental coordination disorder (DCD).

Executive function: Higher levels of brain function, such as paying attention, using the working memory, decision making, planning and setting goals and targets.

Frontal lobes: The front part of the brain responsible for reasoned logical behaviour, initiative, planning and personality.

Glue ear: A condition that can occur in children. The middle ear becomes filled with a thick, sticky fluid as a result of infection; this may result in partial hearing loss. Implicated in dyslexia as sounds (phonemes) are not heard accurately in childhood.

Grommet: Small tube inserted into a child's ear through a small cut in their eardrum. Used to treat glue ear, grommets help drain away fluid from the middle ear and maintain air pressure.

Holistic learner: Likes to see the whole picture before concentrating on the detail.

Interpersonal skills: The ability to relate to others and to work well in group situations.

Intrapersonal skills: The ability to work effectively alone and be self-reliant.

Kinaesthetic learning: Taking in and remembering information by doing – involves moving, handling materials, carrying out experiments.

Long-term memory: Information that is stored for months or years and can be recalled when needed.

Mnemonic: A learning technique using phrases to help remember a spelling or an order of events or things.

Neuron: Nerve cell that receives and transmits information via electrochemical impulses. There are neurons in all parts of the body but they are especially concentrated in the brain.

Neurotransmitters: Special chemicals that transfer impulses from one nerve cell (neuron) to another across tiny gaps called synapses. An example would be dopamine, which is found in the brain. Neurotransmitters are essential for brain function.

Obsessions: Unwanted intrusive thoughts and fears.

Obsessive compulsive disorder (OCD): Experience of recurrent disturbing fears that are irrational and intrusive. Compulsions are an attempt to relieve anxiety by repeating certain actions.

Personal, social and health education (PSHE): This is taught in most schools either as a separate subject or through tutor sessions. Classes emphasise understanding, tolerance and embracing differences.

Personal, social, health and citizenship education (PSHCE): A variant on the term above. Sometimes the 'E' also stands for economic.

Phoneme: A small set of speech sounds that are distinguished by the speakers of a particular language. They can be single letters such as b and p or they can be blends of consonants or vowels such as ch or th or oa. There are 44 phonemes making up the English language.

Phonology: The study of speech sounds in words.

Processing speed: The time taken to absorb information and to think about a response.

Short-term memory (working memory): The ability to remember information for a short while in order to use it. Examples would be remembering a score in a game, a shopping list, or numbers in a maths calculation. The information is then forgotten.

Special educational needs coordinator (SENCO): A teacher who has responsibility for the day-to-day management of special educational needs in a school.

Specific Learning Difficulty (SpLD): A range of problems that some people have in one area of learning while they can perform well or even excel in other areas. It does not affect the overall intelligence of the person.

Synapse: A tiny gap between nerve cells (neurons). Chemicals called neurotransmitters must cross the gap to pass the electrical signal from one nerve cell to the next.

Theory of mind: The ability to see things from someone else's point of view, to understand their behaviour and predict their reactions.

Tic: An involuntary spasm or muscle twitch, often involving face muscles.

Tracking: The ability to coordinate the action of the two eyes to follow a line of print.

Trigger: Something that initiates anxiety and an obsessional thought.

Visual learning: Taking in and remembering information that has been seen.

Visual memory: The ability to remember and recall information that has been seen.

Visual processing: The time it takes to respond to information which has been seen.

Visual stress: A visual problem where the eyes do not work correctly together; can cause print distortion, reading difficulties and headaches. Distance vision can be normal so it is sometimes missed.

Working memory: See short-term memory.

Appendix

Summary table of most common areas of difficulty

	Dyslexia	Dyscalculia	Dysgraphia	Dyspraxia/DCD	ASD /Asperger	ADHD	OCD
Spelling	■						
Reading	■						
Reading comprehension	■				■		
Number confusion		■					
Letter confusion	■						
Symbol confusion	■	■					
Short term memory	■			■		■	
Attention span	■					■	
Poor Organisation		■		■		■	
Gets lost				■	■		
Time keeping				■	■	■	
Likes order / detail					■	■	■
Need to move around				■		■	
Fine coordination			■	■			
Gross coordination				■			
Social skills					■		
Literal translation					■		
Routines / rituals					■		■
Obsessions					■		■
Compulsions							■

Remember, many students will not show all the characteristics listed. Also, some students will have more than one condition.

References and Useful Information

Chapter 1

References

Worthington, A. (ed.) (2003) *The Fulton Special Education Digest.* London: David Fulton Publishers.

Pease, A. and Pease, B. (2001) *Why Men Don't Listen and Women Can't Read Maps.* London: Orion Books Publishers.

Further reading

Brains

Cooper-Kahn, J. and Dietzel, L. (2008) *Late, Lost and Unprepared: A Parent's Guide to Helping Children with Executive Functioning.* Bethesda, MD: Woodbine House Inc. Publishers.

Department for Education and Skills (2005) *SpLD Working Group Guidelines.* 19 July. www.sasc.org.uk

Gathercole, S. and Packiam Alloway, T. (2008) *Working Memory & Learning: A Practical Guide for Teachers.* London: Sage Publications.

Kerchner, G. A. (2014) 'What causes the brain to have slow processing speed, and how can the rate be improved?' *Scientific American Mind* 25, 2, March.

O'Brien, J. and Jones, A. (2004) *The Great Little Book of Brainpower (2nd edn).* England: The Great Little Book Company.

Active and passive learning

NTL. Institute for Applied Behavioral Science. *The Learning Pyramid.* Silver Spring, MD: NTL Institute for Applied Behavioral Science.

Find your own learning style
Howard Gardner's multiple intelligence theories model: www. businessballs.com/howardgardnermultipleintelligences.htm

Learning styles inventory: www.learning-styles-online.com/inventory

The VARK questionnaire: www.vark-learn.com/english/page. asp?p=questionnaire

Glue ear
British Medical Association (2010) *Complete Home Medical Guide (3rd edn).* London: Dorling Kindersley Limited.

'Linking glue ear and dyslexia': www.hi2u.org/Dyslexic/glue_ear_ and_dyslexia.htm

Visual stress
Cerium: www.ceriumoptical.com/vistech/visual-stress.aspx

Worldwide support organisations
USA
National Center for Learning Disabilities (2014) *The State of Learning Disabilities.* New York: NCLD www.ncld.org/wp-content/ uploads/2014/11/2014-State-of-LD.pdf

Australia
Dyslexia SPELD Foundation: 'What is a Specific Learning Disability (SLD)?' http://dsf.net.au/what-are-learning-disabilities

Canada
Learning Disabilities Association of Ontario: www.ldao.ca

New Zealand
SPELD (Specific Learning Difficulties) NZ (New Zealand): www.speld.org.nz

Chapter 2
References
Worthington, A. (ed.) (2003) *The Futon Special Education Digest.* London: David Fulton Publishers.

British Dyslexia Association (undated) 'Dyslexia and specific learning difficulties in adults.' Bracknell: British Dyslexia Association. www.bdadyslexia.org.uk/dyslexic/dyslexia-and-specific-learning-difficulties-in-adults

Schnep, M. H. H. (2014) 'The advantages of dyslexia: with reading difficulties can come other cognitive strengths.' *Scientific American*, 19 August. www.scientificamerican.com/article/the-advantages-of-dyslexia

Further reading

Bennett, J. (2013) *Dyslexia Pocketbook (2nd edn)*. Alresford: Teachers' Pocketbooks.

Goodwin, J. (2012) *Studying with Dyslexia*. London: Palgrave Macmillan.

Grant, D. (2010) *That's the Way I Think: Dyslexia, Dyspraxia and ADHD Explained (2nd edn)*. London: David Fulton Publishers.

Hodge P. (2000) 'A Dyslexic Child in the classroom: A guide for teachers and parents.' www.dyslexia.com/library/classroom.htm

Hornsby B., Shear, F. and Pool J. (1999) *Alpha to Omega (5th edn)*. Oxford: Heinemann.

Hultquist, A. (2006) *An Introduction to Dyslexia for Parents and Professionals*. London: Jessica Kingsley Publishers.

Hultquist, A. (2013) *Can I Tell You About Dyslexia?* London: Jessica Kingsley Publishers.

Pavey B., Meehan, M. and Davis, S. (2013) *The Dyslexia-Friendly Teacher's Toolkit*. London: Sage Publications.

Ott, P. (1997) *How to Detect and Manage Dyslexia*. Oxford: Heinemann.

Reid, G. (2006) *Dyslexia and Inclusion: Classroom Approaches for Assessment, Teaching and Learning*. London: David Fulton Publishers.

Reid, G. and Green, S. (2011) *100 Ideas for Supporting Pupils with Dyslexia*. London: Continuum International Publishing Group.

Resources

Barrington Stoke, a publisher producing books specifically designed for readers with dyslexia. Fast-moving stories, clear text and layout, reading age specific: www.barringtonstoke.co.uk

Crossbow Education, resources such as plastic overlays, reading rulers, software: www.crossboweducation.com

Reading rulers: www.readassist.ic

Fun-with-words, good for mnemonics and other ideas for learning: www.fun-with-words.com

Listening Books, a charity and membership organisation supplying downloads of audio books to individuals for all academic levels. Includes texts for school-level studies and university, both factual and fiction: www.listening-books.org.uk

Animation, showing the differences in the dyslexic brain: http://ncld.org/types-learning-disabilities/dyslexia/the-dyslexic-brain-must-see-video

Technology support

Apps for dyslexia and learning disabilities: http://dyslexiahelp.umich.edu/tools/apps

British Dyslexia Association technology advice website: http://bdatech.org

LexAble Ltd, good resources including Global AutoCorrect program, a spell check designed for dyslexics and based on phonics: www.lexable.com

Texthelp Gold, reading and writing support technology: www.texthelp.com/UK

Wordshark, spelling and reading program: www.wordshark.co.uk/index.aspx

Web links

British Dyslexia Association: www.bdadyslexia.org.uk

Dyslexia Action: www.dyslexiaaction.org.uk

The Dyslexia Association: www.dyslexia.uk.net/contact.html

Helen Arkell Dyslexia Centre, a specialist teaching centre with an excellent information website for teachers: www.arkellcentre.org.uk

Worldwide support organisations

International Dyslexia Association: http://eida.org

USA
American Dyslexia Association: www.american-dyslexia-association.com

Canada
Canadian Dyslexia Association: www.dyslexiaassociation.ca

Australia

Australian Dyslexia Association: http://dyslexiaassociation.org.au

New Zealand

Dyslexia Foundation of New Zealand: www.dyslexiafoundation.org.nz

Chapter 3

References

Department for Education and Skills (2001) *Guidance to Support Pupils with Dyslexia and Dyscalculia. The National Numeracy Strategy.* DfES 0512/2001. London: Department for Education and Skills and Standards and Effectiveness Unit.

British Dyslexia Association (undated) 'Dyscalculia.' www.bdadyslexia. org.uk/dyslexic/dyscalculia

Butterworth, B. (2003) *Dyscalculia Screener.* London: GL Assesment. www.gl-assessment.co.uk/products/dyscalculia-screener

Further reading

Attwood, T. (2013) 'Five ways to understand dyscalculia.' *SEN Magazine,* 64.

Bird, R. (2013) *The Dyscalculia Toolkit: Supporting Learning Difficulties in Maths.* London: Paul Chapman Publishers.

Butterworth, B. and Yeo, D. (2004) *Dyscalculia Guidance: Helping Pupils with Specific Learning Difficulties in Maths.* London: Nelson.

Callaway, E. (2013) 'Dyscalculia: Number games.' *Nature,* 9 January.

Chinn, S. (2011) *The Fear of Maths: How To Overcome It: Sum Hope.* London: Souvenir Press.

Chinn, S. (2012) *The Trouble with Maths (2nd edn).* Abingdon: Routledge.

Chinn, S. and Ashcroft J. R. (2007) *Mathematics for Dyslexics Including Dyscalculia: A Teaching Handbook (3rd edn).* London: Wiley Publishers.

Emerson, J. and Babtie, P. (2014) *The Dyscalculia Solution: Teaching Number Sense.* London: Bloomsbury.

Hannell, G. (2012) *Dyscalculia: Action Plans for Successful Learning in Mathematics.* London: David Fulton Publishers.

Moorcraft, P. (2014) *It Just Doesn't Add Up.* Croydon: Filament Publishing Ltd.

Resources

BDA Technologies Committee, numeracy software for dyslexic learners: http://bdatech.org/learning/i-c-t-numeracy-and-maths/#two

Crossbow Education, good source of materials and games: www.crossboweducation.com/shop-now/maths-teaching-resources

Maths games: www.freeteacher.co.uk

Maths games:www.topmarks.co.uk/maths-games/11-14-years/number

Cambridge House, maths resources and 3D shapes: www.cambridgehouse-dyslexia.co.uk

Wordshark and Numbershark, computer maths games: www.wordshark.co.uk/index.aspx

Numicon, maths resources: www.numicon.co.nz

Special education books on numeracy: www.senbooks.co.uk/view-category/43/Numeracy-and-Dyscalculia

TES (Times Educational Supplement), free maths posters available for teachers: www.tes.co.uk/maths-secondary-teaching-resources

Web links

British Dyslexia Association: www.bdadyslexia.org/uk/dyslexic/dyscalculia

Dyscalculia Support Centre: http://dyscalculiasupportcentre.com

The Dyscalculia Centre: www.dyscalculia.me.uk

The Dyscalculia Centre, teacher resources: www.dyscalculia.me.uk/teacher.html

The Dyscalculia and Dyslexia Interest Group: www.lboro.ac.uk/departments/mec/activities/maths-statistics-support/thedyscalculiaanddyslexiainterestgroup

Steve Chinn, maths author: www.stevechinn.co.uk

Worldwide support organisations

USA

Learning Disabilities Association of America: http://ldaamerica.org/types-of-learning-disabilities/dyscalculia

Canada

Parents Canada: www.parentscanada.com/school/dyscalculia

Australia

Dyscalculia support given by Australian Dyslexia Association: http://dyslexiaassociation.org.au

New Zealand

About Dyscalculia: www.aboutdyscalculia.org/resources.html

Learning and Behavioural Charitable Trust New Zealand: www.lbctnz.co.nz/sld/dyscalculia/index.html

Chapter 4

References

Dyslexia A2Z (undated) 'What is dysgraphia? Dysgraphia symptoms.' www.dyslexiaa2z.com/learning_difficulties/dysgraphia/dysgraphia_what_is.html

American Psychiatric Association (2013) *The Diagnostic and Statistical Manual for Mental Disorders DSM-5.* Arlington, VA: American Psychiatric Publishing.

Further reading

Bennett, J. (2007) *Handwriting Pocketbook.* Alresford: Teachers' Pocketbooks.

Bryce, B. and Stephens, B. (2014) *The Dysgraphia Sourcebook: Everything You Need to Help Your Child.* CreateSpace Independent Publishing Platform.

Sutherland, J. and Green, M. (eds) (2014) *Dysgraphia: Causes, Connections and Cures.* CreateSpace Independent Publishing Platform.

Resources

Crossbow Education, writing aids, pen grips: www.crossboweducation.com/shop-now/handwriting-resources

Back in Action, desk height adjusters, writing slopes, posture packs: www.backinaction.co.uk/computers

Stabilo easy pens, shaped pens for easy writing: www.stabilo.com/uk

Yoropen, ergonomic pens: www.yoropen.com/en/index.html

The Writing Pen Store ergonomic pens and pencils: www.thewritingpenstore.com/c-104-ergonomic-pens-and-pencils.aspx

Assistive technology software

Inclusive Technology: www.inclusive.co.uk/software/dyslexia-software

A range of assistive technology: www.dyslexic.com/software

iansyst, leading assistive technology and disability services supplier: www.iansyst.co.uk

Web links

Best Resources for Achievement and Intervention re Neurodiversity in Higher Education: www.brainhe.com/staff/types/dysgraphiastaff.html

Dyslexia A2Z: www.dyslexiaa2z.com/learning_difficulties/dysgraphia/dysgraphia_what_is.html

'Understanding dysgraphia': www.understood.org/en/learning-attention-issues/child-learning-disabilities/dysgraphia/understanding-dysgraphia

Dyslexia SPELD Foundation: http://dsf.net.au/what-is-dysgraphia

The Good Schools Guide: www.goodschoolsguide.co.uk/help-and-advice/special-needs-advice/types-of-sen/specific-learning-difficulties/192/dysgraphia-difficulty-with-writing

Worldwide support organisations

USA
Handwriting Problem Solutions: www.handwriting-solutions.com/dysgraphia.asp

Canada
Learning Disabilities Association of Ontario:
www.ldao.ca/introduction-to-ldsadhd/ldsadhs-in-depth/articles/about-lds/dysgraphia-the-handwriting-learning-disability

Australia
Dysgraphia support given by the Australian Dyslexia Association: http://dyslexiaassociation.org.au

New Zealand
SPELD (Specific Learning Difficulties) NZ (New Zealand): www.speld.org.nz/dysgraphia.htm

Learning and Behavioural Charitable Trust New Zealand: www.lbctnz.co.nz/sld/dysgraphia/index.html

Chapter 5

References
NHS Choices (undated) 'Developmental co-ordination disorder (dyspraxia) in children.' www.nhs.uk/conditions/dyspraxia-(childhood)/pages/introduction.aspx

Lingam, R., Hunt, L., Golding, J., Jongmans, M. and Emond, A. (2009) 'Prevelance of developmental coordination disorder using the DSM-1V at 7 years of age. A UK population-based study.' *Paediatrics 123*, April, 698–700.

Further reading
Biggs, V. (2005, updated 2014) *Caged in Chaos A Dyspraxic Guide to Breaking Free.* London: Jessica Kingsley Publishers.

Boon, M. (2014) *Can I Tell You About My Dyspraxia?* London: Jessica Kingsley Publishers.

Dixon, D. and Addy, L. (2004) *Making Inclusion Work for Children with Dyspraxia: Practical Strategies for Teachers.* London: Routledge.

Grant, D. (2010) *That's the Way I Think: Dyslexia, Dyspraxia and ADHD Explained (2nd edn).* London: David Fulton Publishers.

Kirby, A. (2009) *Dyspraxia: Developmental and Cooordination Disorder (DCD) (8th edn)*. London: Souvenir Press.

Kirby, A. and Peters, L. (2007) *100 Ideas for Supporting Pupils with Dyspraxia and DCD*. London: Continuum International Publishing Group.

Patrick, A. (2015) *The Dyspraxic Learner: Strategies for Success*. London: Jessica Kingsley Publishers.

Talukdar, A. (2012) *Dyspraxia/DCD Pocketbook*. Alresford: Teachers' Pocketbooks.

Web links

Dyspraxia: secondary school classroom guidelines:
www.dyspraxiafoundation.org.uk/wp-content/uploads/2014/12/a5_dyspraxia_secondary_school_leaflet-indd.pdf

NHS Choices:
www.nhs.uk/conditions/dyspraxia-(childhood)/pages/introduction.aspx

Dyspraxia factsheet:
www.communitychannel.org/uploads/128447393082832/original.pdf

Dyspraxia: www.patient.co.uk/health/Dyspraxia.htm

SpLD Assessment Standards Committee, updated guidance on the assessment of DCD: www.sasc.org.uk/SASCDocuments/Dyspraxia%20guidance%SASC-STEC%Sept%2013.pdf

Resources

Back in Action, desk height adjusters, writing slopes, posture packs: www.backinaction.co.uk/computers

Cambridge House, resources, pencil grips, reading rulers, handwriting pens: www.cambridgehouse-dyslexia.co.uk

Ideas and equipment links: www.boxofideas.org

Yoropen, ergonomic pens: www.yoropen.com/en/index.html

Adapted easi® pens: www.stabilo.com/uk

BBC dance mat typing, touch typing: www.bbc.co.uk/schools/typing

ICT materials

Inclusive Technology:
www.inclusive.co.uk/software/dyslexia-software

A range of assistive technology: www.dyslexic.com/software

Ianyst, leading assistive technology and disability services supplier: www.iansyst.co.uk

Portable Technology Solutions Ltd: http://portabletechnology.co.uk

Web links

Dyspraxia Association of Ireland: www.dyspraxia.ie/teachers

Dyspraxia Connexion: www.dyspraxiaconnexion.org.uk

Dyspraxia Foundation: www.dyspraxiafoundation.org.uk

Movement Matters UK: www.movementmattersuk.org

Worldwide support organisations

USA
Dyspraxia Foundation USA: www.dyspraxiausa.org

Canada
Lexercise: www.lexercise.com

Australia
Dyspraxia Foundation of Australia: www.dyspraxiaaustralia.com.au

New Zealand
The Dyspraxia Support group of New Zealand: www.dyspraxia.org.nz

Chapter 6

NHS Choices (undated) 'Attention deficit hyperactivity disorder (ADHD).' www.nhs.uk/conditions/Attention-deficit-hyperactivity-disorder

American Psychiatric Association (2013) *Diagnostic and Statistical Manual of Mental Disorders, DSM-5 (5th edn)*. Arlington, VA: American Psychiatric Publishing.

Further reading

Grant, D. (2010) *That's the Way I Think: Dyslexia, Dyspraxia and ADHD Explained (2nd edn)*. London: David Fulton Publishers.

Kewley, G. and Latham, P. (2008) *100 Ideas for Supporting Pupils with ADHD*. London: Continuum International Publishing Group.

Kutscher, M. L. (2014) *Kids in the Syndrome Mix of ADHD, LD, Autism Spectrum, Tourette's, Anxiety, and More! (2nd edn)* London: Jessica Kingsley Publishers.

Nunn, T., Hanstock, T. and Lask, B. (2008) *Who's Who of the Brain*. London: Jessica Kingsley Publishers.

O'Regan, F. (2002) *How to Teach and Manage Children with ADHD*. Hyde: LDA Publishers.

O'Regan, F. (2006) *Challenging Behaviours Pocketbook*. Alresford: Teachers' Pocketbooks.

Swietzer, L. (2014) *The Elephant in the ADHD Room*. London: Jessica Kingsley Publishers.

Thompson, A. (2013) *The Boy from Hell: Life with a Child with ADHD* Farringdon: Proof Fairy Publishers.

Web links

ADHD Foundation, provides information and useful video links, leaflets and support for teachers: www.adhdfoundation.org.uk

ADHD Kids, support organisation for parents and children: http://adhdkids.org.uk

ADDISS, the National Attention Deficit Disorder Information and Support Service: www.addiss.co.uk

UK ADHD Partnership, increases awareness among professionals and policy makers, produces information, runs conferences: www.ukadhd.com/index.htm

Web MD, description of executive function and ADHD in teenagers: www.webmd.com/add-adhd/guide/executive-function

Worldwide support organisations

USA

Action Family Foundation: www.actionfamily.org/content/support-groups

Canada

ADDers Canada: www.adders.org/canadamap.htm

Australia

ADDers Australia: www.adders.org/ausmap.htm

New Zealand

ADHD Association: www.adhd.org.nz

Chapter 7

References

American Psychiatric Association (2013) *Diagnostic and Statistical Manual of Mental Disorders, DSM-5 (5th edn)*. Arlington, VA: American Psychiatric Publishing.

Jackson, L. (2002) *Freaks, Geeks and Asperger Syndrome*. London: Jessica Kingsley Publishers.

Further reading

Ansell, G. (2011) *Working with Asperger Syndrome in the Classroom: An Insider's Guide*. London: Jessica Kingsley Publishers.

Attwood, T. (2007) *The Complete Guide to Asperger Syndrome*. London: Jessica Kingsley Publishers.

Attwood, T. (2014) 'Autism Spectrum Disorder Level 1 (Asperger Syndrome) and its treatment.' In M. L. Kutscher, *Kids in the Syndrome Mix of ADHD, LD, Autism Spectrum, Tourette's, Anxiety, and More!* London: Jessica Kingsley Publishers.

Baron-Cohen, S. (2008) *The Facts Autism and Asperger Syndrome*. Oxford: Oxford University Press.

Brower, F. (2007, reprinted 2014) *100 ideas for Supporting Pupils on the Autistic Spectrum*. London: Continuum International Publishing Group.

Schlegelmilch, A. (2014) *Parenting ASD Teens*. London: Jessica Kingsley Publishers.

Stuart-Hamilton, I. (2007) *An Asperger Dictionary of Everyday Expression (2nd edn)*. London: Jessica Kingsley Publishers.

Welton, J. (2004) *What Did You Say? What Did You Mean? An Illustrated Guide to Metaphors*. London: Jessica Kingsley Publishers.

Willey, L. H. (2015) *Pretending to be Normal: Living with Asperger Syndrome (2nd edn)*. London: Jessica Kingsley Publishers.

Winter, M. and Lawrence, C. (2011) *Asperger Syndrome: What Teachers Need to Know*. London: Jessica Kingsley Publishers.

Young, R. (2009 reprinted 2011) *Asperger Syndrome Pocketbook*. Alresford: Teachers' Pocketbooks.

ICT materials

Baron-Cohen, S. (2006) *Mind Reading: The Interactive Guide to Emotions Version 1.3* [CD-ROM – Audiobook]. Cambridge: University of Cambridge.

Web links

ASD visual aids: www.asdvisualaids.com

ASPEN (Autism, Asperger Syndrome Educational Network): www.aspennj.org

Asperger Syndrome Foundation: www.aspergerfoundation.org.uk

National Autistic Society: www.autism.org.uk

Psychcentral, diagnosing ASD quiz: http://psychcentral.com/quizzes/autism.htm

Worldwide support organisations

International Autism Support Network: www.autismsupportnetwork.com

USA

US Autism and Asperger Association: www.usautism.org

American Asperger Association: http://americanaspergers.forumotion.net

Canada

Autism Society Canada: www.autismsocietycanada.ca

Australia

Autism Asperger ACT: www.autismaspergeract.com.au

Autism Spectrum Australia: www.autismspectrum.org.au

New Zealand

Autism New Zealand: www.autismnz.org.nz

Chapter 8

References

Wells, J. (2006) *Touch and Go Joe. An Adolescent's Experience of OCD.* London: Jessica Kingsley Publishers.

Further reading

Jassi, A. (2013) *Can I Tell You About OCD?* London: Jessica Kingsley Publishers.

Kutscher, M. L. (2014) *Kids in the Syndrome Mix of ADHD, LD, Autism Spectrum, Tourette's, Anxiety, and More!* London: Jessica Kingsley Publishers.

Martin, S. and Costello, C. (2008) *The Everything Parent's Guide to Children with OCD.* Fairfield, OH: Adams Media.

Saunders, C. (2015) *Parenting OCD: Down to Earth Advice From One Parent to Another.* London: Jessica Kingsley Publishers.

Woolcock, E. and Campbell, M. (2005) 'The role of teachers in the support of students with obsessive-compulsive disorder.' *The Australian Educational and Developmental Psychologist 22*(1), 54–64.

Support organisations

Mind: www.mind.org.uk/information-support/types-of-mental-health-problems/obsessive-compulsive-disorder-ocd

OCD Action: www.ocdaction.org.uk

OCD-UK: http://ocduk.org

OCD Youth, the site for young people with OCD: http://ocdyouth.org

YoungMinds, mental health in young people: www.youngminds.org.uk

Well at School, supporting young people with mental health problems: www.wellatschool.org

Web links

OCD Education Station: www.ocdeducationstation.org/ocd-facts

Worldwide support organisations

International OCD Foundation, support groups: https://iocdf.org/supportgroups

USA
Anxiety and Depression Association of America, support groups: www.adaa.org/supportgroups

Canada
OCD Ottawa: www.ocdottawa.com

Australia
Reach Out: http://au.reachout.com/obsessive-compulsive-disorder

Sane Australia: www.sane.org/information

New Zealand
Anxiety Support: http://anxietysupport.org.nz

Chapter 9

References

Cambridge University Press (2015) *Cambridge Business English Dictionary*. Cambridge: Cambridge University Press Publishers.

Further reading

Cooper-Kahn, J. and Dietzel, L. (2008) *Late, Lost and Unprepared: A Parent's Guide to Helping Children with Executive Functioning*. Bethesda, MD: Woodbine House Inc. Publishers.

Goodwin, J. (2012) *Studying with Dyslexia*. London: Palgrave Macmillan.

Guare, R., Dawson, P. and Guare, C. (2013) *Smart But Scattered Teens*. New York: Guilford Press.

Ostler, C. and Ward, F. (2012) *Advanced Study Skills (3rd edn)*. Wakefield: SEN Marketing Ltd.

Resources

Apps for dyslexia and learning disabilities: http://dyslexiahelp.umich.edu/tools/apps

British Dyslexia Association technology advice: http://bdatech.org

Cambridge Dictionaries Online: http://dictionary.cambridge.org/dictionary/business-english/organizational-skills

eChalk, a teaching site for teachers: www.echalk.co.uk

EmpTech, many resources including variety of mind mapping and brainstorming programmes: www.emptech.info/index.php

Inspiration, mind mapping software: www.inspiration.com/ie

LexAble Ltd, good resources including Global AutoCorrect program, a spell check designed for dyslexics and based on phonics: www.lexable.com

Texthelp Gold, reading and writing support technology: www.texthelp.com/UK

Chapter 10

Further reading

Pavey B., Meehan, M. and Davis, S. (2013) *The Dyslexia-Friendly Teacher's Toolkit.* London: Sage Publications.

O'Brien, J. and Jones, A. (2004) *The Great Little Book of Brainpower (2nd edn).* England: The Great Little Book Company.

Ostler, C. and Ward, F. (2012) *Advanced Study Skills (3rd edn).* Wakefield: SEN Marketing Ltd.

Exam access arrangement organisations

Joint Council for Qualifications (JCQ) *Access Arrangements, Reasonable Adjustments and Special Considerations 2014–2015 (standard PDF)*: www.jcq.org.uk/exams-office/access-arrangements-and-special-consideration

The SpLD Assessment Standards Committee (SASC) training and practice in the assessment of specific learning difficulties in an educational setting: www.sasc.org.uk

Author biography

Dr Diana Hudson has over 30 years' classroom teaching experience. She has taught in top-ranking schools in the UK in the state and private sectors. She has been a head of biology, head of year and a SENCO (special educational needs coordinator). She has taught adults on Access programmes and first-year medical students. She is a trained teacher of students with Specific Learning Difficulties.

Three of her four children have Specific Learning Difficulties and they have now all successfully negotiated their way through university. Diana has a PhD in Zoology but admits to struggling at school. She was diagnosed as having dyslexia a few years ago.

She is now focusing on increasing teacher awareness of Specific Learning Difficulties and enabling teachers to provide students with the tailored support and encouragement that they need to thrive.

Artist biography

Jon English is a freelance designer, illustrator and photographer based in Sussex in the UK. He enjoys a life of creativity and is never far away from an exciting project, venture or adventure. You can find out more about Jon by visiting www.moomar.co.uk

Index